LEGAL ISSUES OF
CROSS-BORDER
BANKING

LEGAL ISSUES OF CROSS-BORDER BANKING

Edited by Ross Cranston

The Chartered Institute of Bankers

Centre for Commercial Law Studies

Queen Mary College · University of London

First Published 1989

BANKERS BOOKS LIMITED
c/o The Chartered Institute of Bankers
10 Lombard Street
London EC3V 9AS

Chartered Institute of Bankers (CIB) Publications are published by Bankers Books Ltd under an exclusive licence and royalty agreement. Bankers Books Ltd is a company owned by The Chartered Institute of Bankers.

 British Library Cataloguing in Publication Data

Legal issues of cross-border banking. (Cambridge law seminar).
    1. International banking. Law
    I. Cranston, R.
    342.6'8215
ISBN 0 85297 232 6

Typeset in 10/11 pt Times Roman
Text printed on Silverwhite Cartridge
Cover printed on Graphic Strong Bookjacket
by Butler & Tanner Ltd, Frome and London

CONTENTS

TABLE OF STATUTES

National and International Agreements and Directives

TABLE OF CASES

THE CONTRIBUTORS

Ross Cranston—Sir John Lubbock Professor of Banking Law, Queen Mary College, University of London.

Martin Karmel—Senior Deputy Secretary, British Bankers' Association, The Committee of London and Scottish Bankers.

Campbell McLachlan—Solicitor (New Zealand), Herbert Smith, London.

Robert R Pennington—Professor of Commercial Law, University of Birmingham.

Brian Quinn—Assistant Director, Bank of England (appointed Executive Director, April 1988).

John J White—Solicitor, Partner, Cameron Markby, London.

Philip R Wood—Solicitor, Partner, Allen & Overy, London.

ACKNOWLEDGEMENTS

I am grateful to both Alan Miller and Mary Lewis at The Chartered Institute of Bankers for their assistance in organising the seminar on which this book is based and for facilitating its publication. The papers from the seminar are published here with some revisions. (Campbell McLachlan's paper was commissioned subsequent to the seminar to provide a fuller coverage of the subject area.) The Centre for Commercial Law Studies and The Chartered Institute have had a long and fruitful association of which these joint seminars are only one aspect. I should also thank the commentators on the various papers at the seminar: Douglas Bourne, Joe Chubb, Lawrence Collins, Richard Dale, Nick Segal and Richard Youard. Although it has not been possible to publish their comments in this book, the papers have been revised in the light of them.

Thanks are also due to Mary Lewis who copy-edited the manuscript and to Eynon Smart and Anne Lyons who prepared the Tables of Statutes and Cases and the Subject Index.

This is the first joint seminar in which Professor R M Goode FBA has not participated. (He was on sabbatical leave in the United States at the time.) These seminars were Roy Goode's idea and he has done much to promote the study of banking law in the University of London and to foster links with the Institute. It is appropriate to pay tribute to his work in this regard.

INTRODUCTION

Ross Cranston

Cross-border banking has raised a number of legal problems over the years. In recent times, however, the range has increased and the problems have become more acute. Fraud involving the use of the international banking system is one important cause, but others include international concern about the stability and competitive equality of banking and financial systems. The Sixth Banking Law Seminar, organised by The Chartered Institute of Bankers and the Centre for Commercial Law Studies at Queen Mary College, University of London, held in November 1987, was devoted to exploring some of these legal problems in cross-border banking, mainly from the perspective of English law. What follows is an, albeit brief, attempt to provide a framework for considering these problems. The book touches on the major themes of the papers presented at the seminar, some of the points raised in the discussion and other issues relevant to the topic.

PRIVATE LAW

The law relating to cross-border banking is still mainly private law. In many areas the relevant rules are fairly clear, although there are some important grey areas. Legislation is intruding increasingly on the rules of private law, in some cases as a result of international measures.

(a) Institutional arrangements

The legal analysis of cross-border banking arrangements turns on the principles of agency and legal personality. Cross-border banking can be carried on by a correspondent, representative office (now defined for the purposes of the Banking Act 1987[1]), a branch, or a subsidiary. The first involves an agency relationship, the last an independent entity in English law. There are indications, however, that the latter might not insulate completely the head office of a

1. s. 74(3).

bank. In *Idmac Industrial Designers and Management Consultants BV* v *Midland Bank Ltd*[2], Templeman LJ commented that it was high time that the clearing banks looked very carefully at their subsidiaries in other jurisdictions to ensure that there was no longer any scope for them being used as a cloak for fraud. Using cases like *Gilford Motors Company Ltd* v *Horne*[3] and *Wallersteiner* v *Moir (No. 1)*[4], a court might ignore the separate corporate form of a banking subsidiary where that is used as a cloak for fraud. In practice, the Bank of England requires foreign banks to give letters of comfort in relation to their subsidiaries in Britain.

What of a branch? Certainly for authorisation purposes under the Banking Act 1987 it is treated separately. In *R* v *Grossman*[5], Lord Denning MR treated a branch as a different entity separate from its head office. However, as Staughton J said in *Libyan Arab Foreign Bank* v *Bankers Trust Company*[6], a branch is a separate entity for some purposes only. The problem is to identify which those purposes are.

(b) Banking law

There are some well established principles of banking law relevant in the cross-border context. One is the bank's obligation of confidentiality to its customers—see the *Tournier* principle[7] discussed in the papers by John White and Martin Karmel. Others are outlined in my paper on the freezing and expropriation of bank deposits. One is the cardinal principle that the obligation of a bank to its customer is in general that of a debtor to its creditor. Another is that the place of performance of a bank's obligation to repay a deposit is at the branch where the deposit is held.

(c) Conflicts of law

The principles of conflicts of law are clearly central to any discussion of cross-border banking. As Professor Pennington points out in his paper *Court orders affecting foreign bank deposits*, they determine whether the courts of the country have jurisdiction to decide disputes about the rights and obligations of the bank and the customer as regards each other, what rules of law must be applied to resolve such

2. *The Times*, 8 October 1981.
3. [1933] Ch 935.
4. [1974] 1 WLR 991; [1974] 3 All ER 217.
5. (1981) 73 CAR 302, 307.
6. [1987] 2 FTLR 509, 522; [1988] 1 Lloyd's Rep 259, 271.
7. *Tournier* v *National Provincial and Union Bank of England* [1924] 1 KB 461.

disputes, and where the bank balance must be treated as situate so as to be subject to the claims of third persons. The English courts have used alternate solutions to determine the system of law governing a bank account. One is to look at the place where the account is kept at the relevant time, the other to decide the residence of the debtor (the bank or customer, as the case may be). The former was favoured in *Libyan Arab Foreign Bank* v *Bankers Trust Company*[8].

(d) Jurisdiction

Professor Pennington also explores the two sets of rules to determine whether an English court will regard itself as having jurisdiction in respect of a bank account where there is a foreign element. The first set derives from the 1968 Convention on Jurisdiction and the Enforcement of Judgments in Civil and Commercial Matters, which applies primarily to members of the European Economic Community[9], and the second derives from sources such as the Rules of the Supreme Court, Order 11, which is relevant when there is a foreign element but the Convention does not apply.

(e) Remedies

Remedies in cross-border banking fall, in important respects, into the category of self-help. The default clause in a loan agreement, and the right of set-off are well known examples. Self-help looms large because of practical advantages such as speed and the legal, and other, uncertainties surrounding the alternative of invoking the judicial machinery. Yet these self-help remedies are not legally clear cut; in cross-border banking this is compounded by the conflict of laws problems to which they give rise. Philip Wood's paper, *Set-off and the conflict of laws*, is a masterly attempt to resolve some of these legal difficulties in relation to set-off. He begins with an innovative, but convincing, classification of the types of set-off, before considering the relevant conflict of law rules. While concentrating on English law, there is reference to the rules of other legal systems.

Judicial remedies in the context of cross-border banking are various. Obtaining information about a person's financial affairs may require evidence about his or her bank account in another jurisdiction. Letters of request or letters rogatory under the Hague Convention on Jurisdiction and the Enforcement of Judgments in Civil and Commercial Matters 1968 are one method of doing this.

8. [1987] 2 FTLR 509, 521; [1988] 1 Lloyd's Rep 259, 270–1.
9. See Peter Kaye, *Civil Jurisdiction and Enforcement of Foreign Judgments*, Abingdon, Oxon, Professional Books, 1987.

3

English courts do not automatically accede to such requests, however, and in making a decision balance the public interest of assisting foreign courts with factors such as the undesirability of fishing expeditions and a banker's obligation of confidentiality to customers[10]. A subpoena is another method of obtaining evidence about a bank account in another jurisdiction. If objection is taken to a bank's complying with a foreign subpoena, an English court will identify the proper law of the account and, if the proper law is English, restrain the bank from breaching confidentiality in the absence of overwhelming factors supporting it[11].

In tracing assets through the international banking system, other remedies are relevant, although of variable effectiveness. Discovery, the *Mareva* injunction, the Bankers' Books Evidence Act 1879, and the ancient writ of *ne exeat regno* have all featured in recent English decisions[12]. Moreover, a judgment in one jurisdiction may be enforceable in another jurisdiction[13].

THE INTERSECTION OF PRIVATE AND PUBLIC LAW

In some of the areas already considered, legislation has had an impact on issues mainly in matters of private law. In the area addressed in Martin Karmel's paper, the sources of bank deposits, the impact of legislation has been, and will be, quite profound. After a few remarks about that topic, it is worthwhile to say something about how, as a matter of policy, legislating in such areas ought to be approached.

(a) The sources of bank deposits
Legislation in the form of s. 4, Cheques Act 1957 has given banks an incentive to vet new customers. This section protects a collecting bank from claims in conversion, if its customer does not have title to certain instruments, notably cheques, and if it acts without negligence. The courts have held that, to act without negligence for the purposes of the section, banks must vet new customers[14]. Martin

---

10. In re *Westinghouse Electric Corporation Uranium Contract Litigation MDL docket No. 235* [1978] AC 547; In re *State of Norway's Application* [1987] QB 433.
11. *X AG* v *A Bank* [1983] 2 All ER 464.
12. e.g. *Bankers Trust Co.* v *Shapira* [1980] 1 WLR 1274; *Ashtiani* v *Kashi* [1987] QB 888; *Mckinnon* v *Donaldson, Lufkin and Jenrette Securities Corp* [1986] Ch 482; *Al Nahkel for Contracting and Trading Ltd* v *Lowe* [1986] QB 235.
13. The English rules are dealt with in *Dicey & Morris The Conflict of Laws*, 11th ed., 1987, chs 14–15.
14. e.g. *Lumsden & Co.* v *London Trustee Savings Bank* [1971] 1 Lloyd's Rep 114.

Karmel points to comparable provisions in other countries.

Section 24 of the Drug Trafficking Offences Act 1986 means that there is a possibility that a bank could be criminally responsible for assisting drug traffickers, although it does not commit a crime if it reports its suspicion or belief to the police. Disclosure in such cases is treated as not being in breach of the banker's duty of confidentiality. Section 98 of the Criminal Justice Act 1988 provides that disclosure to the police in relation to property obtained in connection with a range of serious offences shall not be treated as a breach of confidence. Both s. 24 and s. 98 refer to a duty imposed by contract; the *Tournier* decision established clearly that the banker's duty of confidence is imposed as a matter of implied contract[15]. Such legislation has been a feature of the scene in the United States for some years. The Bank Secrecy Act 1970 required banks to submit reports to the Internal Revenue Service regarding relatively large transactions. There has been a dramatic increase in the number of reports filed following the well publicised prosecution of the Bank of Boston in 1985. The Money Laundering Control Act makes the act of money laundering itself illegal, thereby greatly increasing the potential liability of bank officials[16].

The importance of legislation in this area, however, should not blind us to the continued vitality of private law. The rules about constructive trusts are relevant to the issue of the sources of bank deposits. A third party, such as a bank, may be liable for having knowingly assisted a breach of trust—the second limb of Lord Selborne's famous statement in *Barnes* v *Addy*[17]. There are still uncertainties as to the scope of such liability. Is it confined to breaches of trust, or does it extend to breaches of fiduciary obligations? Does 'knowingly assisting' encompass constructive knowledge of the breach? Is the lynch pin of liability whether there is a lack of probity on the part of the third-party bank? We do not need to answer these questions here, but it is clear that in appropriate cases, liability will be imposed on a bank as a constructive trustee.

In one of the most recent decisions, *Lipkin Gorman* v *Karpnale Ltd*[18], although Alliot J held that something more than constructive knowledge was required for liability, he held that the bank was liable in this case since the manager of the relevant branch had either shut

---

15. At pp. 471–2, 480, 484.
16. See F Knecht, *Extraterritorial Jurisdiction and the Federal Money Laundering Offense* (1986) 22 *Stanford J Int L* 389.
17. (1874) 9 Ch App 244, 252.
18. [1987] 1 WLR 987.

his eyes to the obvious, or wilfully and recklessly failed to make proper enquiries as to the source of the customer's funds. The manager knew about the customer's gambling habit and he had misled the partner of the customer's law firm about it. '[H]is conduct is only explicable upon the basis that he was shutting his eyes to the obvious source of [the customer's] money to gamble with, or was wilfully and recklessly failing to make such inquiries as a reasonable and honest man would make'[19].

(b) Legislative change

Legislation needs systematic thought; an ad hoc response to a particular problem may not be the best way of dealing with it. Take the rule about bank confidentiality. As already mentioned, the rule has been modified in relation to drugs trafficking. The Criminal Justice Act 1988 modifies the rule about bank confidentiality still further for a wider range of offences. Yet, a fundamental re-appraisal of the rule itself might lead us to support one of the suggestions put forward in John White's paper, that the rule be abolished altogether. After all, the general doctrine of confidentiality had rather inauspicious beginnings, being conceived by Prince Albert's private etchings, the recipe for Morison's *Universal Medicine* and Dr Abernethy's lectures in surgery[20]. Underlying the doctrine are conflicting policies, as in the area of banking, where the privacy of the individual customer, and the need to maintain commercial secrecy on the part of the commercial customer, conflicts with the uncovering and punishment of fraud and crime. In any event, why should the law protect privacy in this respect, when generally it does not do so? It is easy to see the social ends with information about private and sexual activities in the hands of spouses and doctors—we wish to preserve marital relationships and want to prevent abuse by those in positions of dominance—but what of bank confidentiality? In the *Tournier* decision, Bankes LJ gave as a reason that the 'credit of the customer depends very largely upon the strict observance of that confidence'[21]. In *R v Grossman*, Lord Denning referred to the private interest in keeping a bank account confidential[22], and privacy seemed to be at the base of Kerr LJ's approach in *In re Norway's Application*[23]— neither reason is impervious to argument.

19. At p. 1012.
20. P D Finn, *Confidentiality and the 'Public Interest'* (1984) 58 *ALJ*, 497. I have drawn on this paper for some of the following.
21. [1924] 1 KB 461, 474.
22. (1981) 73 Cr App R 302, 307.
23. [1987] QB 433, 485, 487.

INTERNATIONAL MEASURES

Expropriation of bank deposits or a bank's assets will have international repercussions if a holder of those deposits is outside the state or if the assets are owned by a bank based outside that state. The same may apply in the event of a moratorium being imposed on the repayment of a bank deposit or exchange control being introduced. My own paper *The freezing and expropriation of bank deposits* explores the relevant English law regarding these matters, and also examines how an English court will treat a freeze imposed by another jurisdiction on the repayment of deposits in England by persons associated with that jurisdiction.

Domestic legislation has already been referred to, for example, the Drug Trafficking Offences Act 1986, which has had an impact on cross-border banking. No more need be said of this here.

At the international public law level, there are the various steps described by Brian Quinn in his paper on the cross-border regulation of banking. At the bilateral level there are the attempts, such as the United States–United Kingdom capital adequacy proposal, issued in 1987, as a result of discussions between the Bank of England and United States authorities[24]. Multilateral approaches include the work of the Cook Committee, including its work on this topic[25]. These are outlined in Brian Quinn's paper. In addition, there are the measures to facilitate international enforcement: most notable is the United States–Swiss Mutual Legal Assistance Treaty[26].

24. *Agreed Proposal of the United States Federal Banking Supervisory Authorities and the Bank of England on Primary Capital and Capital Adequacy Assessment* (1987).
25. Bank of International Settlements, Committee on Banking Regulations and Supervisory Practices, *Proposals for International Convergence of Capital Measurement and Capital Standards* (1987).
26. The text is at (1973) 12 *International Legal Materials* 916. Subsequent understandings are at (1976) 15 ibid. 283; (1983) 22 ILML; (1988) 27 ibid. 480.

7

PRINCIPLES OF CONFIDENTIALITY IN CROSS-BORDER BANKING

John J White

Introduction

Most jurisdictions recognise, in some form or other, that a bank owes a duty of confidentiality to its customer. In the United Kingdom the duty arises out of contract and is subject to the qualifications defined by Bankes L J in *Tournier* v *National Provincial and Union Bank of England*[1]. The qualifications are well known to bankers but are worth restating as they run like threads through the relevant case law. Disclosure is permissible:

(a) under compulsion by law;
(b) where there is a duty to the public to disclose;
(c) where the interests of the bank require disclosure;
(d) where the disclosure is made with the express or implied consent of the customer.

Australia, Hong Kong and some other common law jurisdictions have adopted the principles enunciated in the Tournier case. By contrast Switzerland[2], the Bahamas[3] and other tax- and money-haven jurisdictions impose or buttress the duty by statute so that contravention gives rise to criminal, as well as civil, proceedings. Inevitably a court asked to grant a disclosure order taking effect in another jurisdiction, or considering the effect under its local law, of a disclosure order made by a court in another jurisdiction, will have regard to the provisions of its local law governing disclosure.

The pressure for easier disclosure is increasing as states seek to trace and recover the proceeds of crimes committed within their jurisdiction (drug offences, tax evasion, insider trading offences, etc.)

---

1. [1924] 1 KB 461, CA.
2. Federal Law Relating to Banks and Saving Banks of 8 November 1934, as amended in 1971, Art. 47.
3. Bank and Trust Companies Regulation Act 1965 and the Confidential Relationships (Preservation Law) of 1976.

and remitted abroad. The present attempt by the United States Department of Justice to trace funds diverted by President Marcos of the Philippines into various Swiss and Hong Kong bank accounts, in particular accounts with Barclays Bank plc in Hong Kong, may not, unfortunately, result in a leading case giving guidance on the issues considered by this paper as every effort is being made to resolve the problem at the political level. However it is difficult to escape the conclusion, in any review of the principles of confidentiality in cross-border banking, that it is a case of 'USA v The Rest'.

Viscount Dilhorne, in *In re Westinghouse Electric Corp. Uranium Contract Litigation MDL Docket No. 235*[4], felt constrained to say:

'For many years now the United States has sought to exercise jurisdiction over foreigners in respect of acts done outside the jurisdiction of that country. This is not in accordance with international law. . .'[5]

In *Mackinnon v Donaldson Lufkin and Jenrette Securities Corp.*[6], Hoffmann J underlined the regrettable conflict with the United States by remarking, when considering the principle that a state should refrain from demanding obedience to its sovereign authority by foreigners in respect of their conduct outside the jurisdiction:

'It is perhaps ironic that the most frequent insistence on this principle by Her Majesty's Government has been as a result of its violation by the courts and government agencies of the United States'.[7]

Against that background what principles can be detected?

GRANT OF DISCLOSURE ORDERS PURPORTING TO HAVE EXTRATERRITORIAL EFFECT

The English courts have been extremely reluctant to grant disclosure orders intended to take effect in other jurisdictions. In *R v Grossman*[8],

4. [1978] AC 547.
5. At p. 631.
6. [1986] 1 All ER 653.
7. At p. 658.
8. (1981) 73 Cr App R 302, CA.

the Inland Revenue wished to obtain evidence of tax evasion against a Mr Grossman. It was alleged that he had paid the proceeds of the tax evasion into the account of a company controlled by him with an Isle of Man bank—Savings & Investment Bank Limited (SIB) which maintained its own accounts with the Isle of Man branch of Barclays Bank. The Inland Revenue obtained an ex parte order from the High Court in England under the Bankers Books Evidence Act 1879 which was directed to the head office of Barclays in London and required Barclays to permit copies to be taken of the entries in the books of its Isle of Man branch relating to the particular account of SIB suspected to contain the proceeds of the tax evasion. The Inland Revenue had previously applied to the Deemster in the Isle of Man for a disclosure order under the Manx Bankers Books Evidence Act 1935 but had been refused in forthright terms. The matter came before the Court of Appeal on an application by SIB to discharge the order. Lord Denning MR, giving the leading judgment, accepted that the court had power to order the head office of Barclays to produce the books but that the discretion of the court should not be exercised to require such production because of the danger of a conflict of jurisdictions between the High Court of England and the Manx courts. He said, and this appears to be a guiding principle:

'... that is a conflict which we must always avoid.'[9]

The next, and most recent, authority is the judgment of Hoffmann J in the *Mackinnon* case[10]. Mr Mackinnon alleged fraud against two individuals who had paid the proceeds of the fraud into the account of a Bahamian company at Citibank, New York. He obtained a subpoena and an ex parte order under the Bankers Books Evidence Act 1879 directed to the London branch of Citibank requiring it to produce the books and other papers held at its head office in New York relating to transactions which took place in New York on the account maintained there by the Bahamian company. Citibank applied to have the subpoena and the order set aside. This, Hoffman J agreed to do, on the basis that disclosure orders of this kind should not be made save in very exceptional circumstances and that such circumstances had not been demonstrated by Mr Mackinnon. He was able to come to this view notwithstanding that counsel for Citibank could not contend that disclosure would violate any law of New York (thus distinguishing the *Grossman* decision where dis-

9. At p. 308.
10. *Mackinnon* v *Donaldson Lufkin and Jenrette Securities Corp.* [1986] 1 All ER 653.

closure would have contravened Manx law) because the Bahamian company had long since been dissolved as a defunct company and any duty of confidence likely to be owed under New York law had ceased to exist. He came to the conclusion that there were no 'exceptional circumstances', first, because there was an alternative remedy available to Mr Mackinnon, namely an application to the courts of New York and, secondly, because it was not a case of 'hot pursuit'.

The indication that Hoffman J would regard 'hot pursuit' as an exceptional circumstance is interesting. It refers to an unreported judgment of Templeman J in *London & Counties Securities* v *Caplan*[11], in which he ordered an English bank to procure from its overseas banking subsidiaries documents relating to accounts connected with Mr Caplan in order to trace assets which he was said to have embezzled. The exceptional circumstances in that case were, first, that it was one of crime and fraud and, secondly, that 'unless effective relief is granted, justice may well become impossible because the evidence and the fruits of crime and fraud may disappear'.

The principles to be divined from these cases appear to be that the English courts will not make a disclosure order having extra-territorial effect if:

(a) disclosure would contravene the law of the relevant foreign state. Unfortunately, the cases do not make clear whether the contravention has to be such as to give rise to criminal penalties or whether a contravention giving rise to a mere breach of a contractual duty of secrecy, leading to a damages claim and/or a mandatory order and committal for contempt, would be sufficient. This principle is at least analogous with the rule of private international law that contractual performance will not be enforced if it is illegal under the law of the place of performance;

(b) even though disclosure would not contravene the law of the relevant foreign state, there are no exceptional circumstances such as hot pursuit or lack of any other available remedies.

The position in the United States is very different, albeit confusing. The basic weapons available to the American courts are the subpoena, if oral evidence is required and the subpoena *duces tecum*, if production of documents is required. A bank or a bank official

11. 26 May 1978.

refusing to comply faces contempt proceedings. Early indications were promising. In 1958 the Supreme Court refused to order a Swiss bank to make disclosures which would have contravened Swiss bank law[12] and in 1959 a foreign law prohibiting disclosure was held to be sufficient to defeat an application for a disclosure order[13]. However, attitudes then began to harden and subsequent decisions made it clear that, if an application for a disclosure order was to be refused, the foreign law prohibition on disclosure either had to be absolute or conditional on permission and, if the latter, the bank against which the disclosure order was sought had to demonstrate to the court's satisfaction that it had made bona fide attempts to obtain the necessary consent[14].

There followed two cases in the early 1980s which are difficult to distinguish although the United States courts succeeded in doing so. In *US* v *The Bank of Nova Scotia*[15], a Federal grand jury issued a subpoena *duces tecum* in connection with a tax and narcotics investigation of a United States citizen requiring production of certain records held at the Bahamian branch of the Bank of Nova Scotia. The Bank of Nova Scotia refused to comply on the grounds that s.10 of the Bahamian Bank and Trust Companies Regulation Act 1965 prohibited disclosure without consent and imposed criminal sanctions for unauthorised disclosure. The 11th Circuit Court of Appeals held that the bank had not satisfied a test of good faith because it had not sought the consent of the Bahamian authorities. The bank also contended that comity between nations precluded enforcement of the subpoena which forced the court to apply the balancing test provided in the United States Restatement (2nd) of Foreign Relations Law 1965. This provides that a United States court should consider moderating the exercise of its jurisdiction, in considering whether or not to order a party to act contrary to the law of another State to which he is also subject, by taking into account a number of factors including:

(a) the vital national interest of each of the states;
(b) the hardship that inconsistent enforcement actions would impose upon the party;

---

12. *Société Internationale Pour Participations Industrielles et Commerciales SA* v *Rogers*, 357 US 197 (1958).
13. *First National City Bank* v *IRS*, 271 F2d 616 (1959).
14. e.g. *US* v *First National City Bank*, 396 F2d 897 (1968); and *SEC* v *Banca Della Svizzera Italiana*, 92 FRD 111 (1981).
15. 691 F2d 1384 (1982).

(c) the extent to which the required conduct is to take place in the territory of the other state;
(d) the nationality of the party;
(e) the extent to which enforcement by action of either state can reasonably be expected to achieve compliance.

The court found that the United States interest in the case, namely the stemming of the narcotics trade, was of paramount importance and that, accordingly, the balance of interest came down on the side of ordering the bank to comply with the subpoena.

In the second case, *US v First National Bank of Chicago*[16], the Internal Revenue Service (IRS) obtained a disclosure order in the United States courts against the First National Bank of Chicago requiring production in the United States of bank statements of a customer whose account was held at the Athens branch of the bank. The bank refused to comply on the grounds that disclosure would expose its employees to penal sanctions under the Greek Bank Secrecy Act. When the matter came before the 7th Circuit Court of Appeals the court applied the 'balance-of-interest' approach derived from the Restatement (2nd) of Foreign Relations Law and concluded that it would be an abuse of its discretion to permit the disclosure order to stand unqualified as the balance of interest came down on the side of the bank. It therefore ordered the bank to make a 'good faith' effort to obtain permission from the relevant Greek authorities to produce the required information and indicated that if the bank could demonstrate that it had made such a 'good faith' effort, but had failed, the disclosure order would not be enforced. The court distinguished the *Bank of Nova Scotia* case because (a) the information sought by the grand jury in the *Bank of Nova Scotia* case concerned a tax *and* a narcotics investigation whereas in the *First National Bank of Chicago* case the investigation was merely in furtherance of a tax gathering exercise; and (b) Bahamian law was different from Greek law in that disclosure with the consent of the customer was not a criminal offence under Bahamian law whereas it was under Greek law. The latter ground of distinguishment is particularly difficult to follow as the issue of the customer's consent does not appear to have been raised in either case, it being naturally assumed that the consent of the customer would be the last thing that either bank would be able to obtain.

Finally, on the case law, two decisions of the New York District Court in March 1984: *Garpeg Limited and The Chase Manhattan*

16. 699 F2d 341 (1983).

Bank NA v *US* and *US* v *The Chase Manhattan Bank NA*[17] both applied the balance-of-interest test provided by the Restatement (2nd) of Foreign Relations Law. Both cases involved Gucci shops, the Gucci family, Chase Manhattan and the suspicions of the IRS that the Gucci family had made large payments to Hong Kong companies with bank accounts at the Hong Kong branch of Chase Manhattan categorised as management charges but really intended to reduce the Gucci family's taxable income in the United States. In both cases the IRS obtained disclosure orders against the bank's head office in New York requiring production of its records held in Hong Kong. The Hong Kong companies obtained interim injunctions in Hong Kong against the bank restraining disclosure. Accordingly, the matters came before the New York courts as an application by the bank for an order discharging the disclosure order, or alternatively requiring the Hong Kong companies to discontinue proceedings in the Hong Kong courts, to waive their secrecy rights and to consent to the required disclosure and an application by the IRS to enforce the disclosure order. The courts found that the enforcement of United States tax laws was unquestionably of vital interest to the United States and that outweighed the interest of Hong Kong in maintaining its banking secrecy doctrine which was essentially a commercial matter founded in contract (Hong Kong having adopted the *Tournier* principles) rather than a statutory obligation of more concern to the Hong Kong government. The fact that the investigation was 'merely' for tax purposes did not sway the courts as it had, apparently, in the *First National Bank of Chicago* case.

The attitude of the United States courts appears to be hardening all the time. The relatively recent introduction of the balance-of-interest test which should, at first blush, have assisted the banks, has not actually done so because the courts have had regard primarily to the first factor to be taken into account, namely the vital national interest of each of the states involved, and, unsurprisingly, in the majority of cases, have decided that the vital national interest of the United States outweighed the vital national interest of the other state concerned. Tax gathering is more vital to the United States than observance of injunctions granted by its courts is to Hong Kong.

There is a plain contrast between the stance of the English courts, with their strict observance of the relevant rules of international law as they perceive them and their respect for the comity of nations, and the stance of the United States courts ever eager to extend the

---

17. (1984) 84–US Tax Cases.

extraterritorial effect of their orders. John Spender and Gregory Burton refer to the attitude of the United States courts as 'judicial xenophobia'[18] and it remains to be seen whether a cure can be found for that painful (to others) disease.

ACCEPTANCE OF ORDERS PURPORTING TO HAVE EXTRATERRITORIAL EFFECT

Although the English courts have been hesitant to grant orders having extraterritorial effect, they have been far more resolute in defending the national interest against the effect of orders of the United States courts. In the leading case of *X AG v A Bank*[19], the anonymous plaintiff was a Swiss company and the anonymous defendant an American bank with a branch in London at which the plaintiff company maintained its accounts. Although only one company in the group, of which the plaintiff was the parent, had any dealings in the United States, the Department of Justice sought information concerning all members of the group in connection with an investigation into the crude oil industry. A subpoena was served on the head office of the defendant bank in the United States for production in the United States of its banking records held in London relating to the plaintiff company and its subsidiaries. The plaintiff company obtained interim injunctions in the High Court in England restraining the defendant bank from producing the records requested and the Department of Justice then obtained an ex parte order in the New York District Court requiring the defendant bank to comply with the subpoena. Accordingly, the matter came before Leggatt J as an application by the plaintiff company for an order to continue the interim injunctions granted in England. As Leggatt J pointed out, the dilemma was present in its acutest form. The defendant bank was subject in the United States to a subpoena supported by a compulsion order of a competent court of the United States whilst, at the same time, being restrained by injunctions granted by a competent court in England prohibiting it from complying with the subpoena. The judge had no difficulty in finding that the customer–banker relationship was governed by English law and hence the *Tournier* principles applied. Leggatt J found for the plaintiff company

---

18. *Aspects of Conflict of Laws in Banking Transactions* (1987) 61, *Australian Law Journal*, 65, 73.
19. [1983] 2 All ER 464.

and continued the injunctions on the basis of the balance of convenience. He concluded:

> 'I can summarise in a sentence the balance of convenience as I see it. On the one hand there is involved the continuation of the injunctions impeding the exercise by the United States court in London of powers which, by English standards, would be regarded as excessive, without in so doing causing detriment to the bank: on the other hand the refusal of the injunctions, or the non-continuation of them, would cause potentially very considerable commercial harm to the plaintiffs, which cannot be disputed, by suffering the bank to act for its own purposes in breach of the duty of confidentiality admittedly owed to its customers.'[20]

Although Leggatt J considered that the balance of convenience tipped in favour of the plaintiff company on a number of grounds, the principal reason appears to be his acceptance of expert evidence as to the position in the United States given on behalf of the plaintiff company. That expert evidence averred that it was highly unlikely that a United States bank or its officers would be held in contempt for conduct complying with the order of an English court in the circumstances of the case: that is an injunction restraining the transfer or disclosure of records kept in London in respect of a bank account maintained by a non-American corporation at the bank's London branch. The expert witness declared himself quite certain 'that no United States court has ever held a bank or other party in contempt in such circumstances' assuming as he did, that there is no suggestion of wrongdoing by the bank, either in transferring overseas records ordinarily kept in New York, or in any way assisting in a scheme of concealment or non-disclosure. This constitutes the United States doctrine of foreign government compulsion. Put briefly, in the circumstances of the *X AG* case, it means that a United States court would not dare to hold a party in contempt of one of its orders if compliance with that order would put that party in contempt of an order of an English court. Suffice it to say that the cases referred to above do not demonstrate such sensitivity on the part of the United States courts.

In re State of Norway's Application[21], involved the Court of Appeal considering letters of request issued by Norway seeking the assistance of the English court in connection with a deceased

20. At p. 480.
21. [1987] QB 433.

Norwegian taxpayer who, it was alleged, had evaded Norwegian tax by secretly transferring a substantial part of his assets to a Panamanian company, the shares of which were owned by a trust which kept its bank accounts at Lazard Brothers. Specifically the letters of request sought the examination, as witnesses, of two officials of Lazards under the Evidence (Proceedings in Other Jurisdictions) Act 1975. The application for oral examination was granted ex parte, the witnesses appealed to McNeill J who dismissed their appeal and the witnesses then came to the Court of Appeal. There were a number of issues in dispute but the principal one of concern to this paper is whether, in all the circumstances of the case, the witnesses should be ordered to break their duty of confidentiality. On that issue all three judges agreed that, of the four qualifications to the banker's duty of confidentiality specified in the *Tournier* decision, the only applicable qualification was that of public duty, and that the court had to carry out a balancing exercise weighing the desirability of assisting a foreign court against the upholding of the duty of confidentiality. Two judges agreed that in appropriate circumstances the importance of assisting a foreign court would outweigh the banker's obligation of secrecy but that such circumstances had not been established in the instant case. Those two judges appear to have reached that conclusion on the basis that the information sought by the letters of request was so wide as to be a 'fishing expedition' and it would not be right to order bankers to break their duty of secrecy to assist fishermen. The third judge took a different view, in somewhat equivocal terms, suggesting that the court should exercise its discretion by applying the principle that a witness whose evidence was sought by a foreign court should be directed to answer no more and no less than would be required of him in proceedings in the English courts. It is understood that this case is presently under appeal to the House of Lords.

The third case for consideration is the other side of the coin of the *Chase Manhattan* cases referred to above. A disclosure order, obtained by the IRS, had been served on the head office of Chase Manhattan in the United States requiring it to disclose banking records held in its Hong Kong branch relating to Hong Kong corporations (*FDC Co. Limited, Vanguard International Manufacturing Limited Inc., Garpeg Limited* v *The Chase Manhattan Bank NA*). The matter came before the Hong Kong Court of Appeal on an appeal by Chase Manhattan against injunctions granted by a judge in chambers restraining disclosure sought by the IRS. The Court of Appeal was swift and forthright in its defence of the banking secrecy laws in Hong Kong. Huggins VP observed:

'All persons opening accounts with banks in Hong Kong, whether foreign or local banks, are entitled to look to the Hong Kong courts to enforce any obligation of secrecy which, by the law of Hong Kong, is implied by virtue of the relationship of banker and customer.'[22]

The court was sympathetic to the bank's position but declined to concern itself with the possibility of the bank being subject to contempt proceedings in the United States, holding that the matter was outside its competence and irrelevant for the purposes of its own decision. This was a very different view from that taken by Leggatt J in *X AG* v *A Bank* and suggests a more robust, colonial approach to the predatory effect of United States court orders.

The conclusions to be drawn from these three cases appear to be that the English courts, and courts in jurisdictions which tend to follow English lines of judicial thinking, will continue to defend their local law requirements of banking confidentiality either by an outright refusal to accept the extraterritorial effect of the orders of courts of other jurisdictions, or by a more sophisticated analysis of the legal principles involved. In other jurisdictions, where banking secrecy is protected by statute, more commercial considerations prevail but lead to the same result. For example, Caribbean countries which have introduced banking secrecy and tax-haven laws in order to attract an inward flow of funds will not easily surrender that commercial advantage by bowing to the weight of orders issued by the courts of other jurisdictions.

STATUTES, TREATIES AND CONVENTIONS

Cross-border confidentiality has only received legislative attention comparatively recently and then only in the wider context of obtaining evidence overseas generally. Thus, the Evidence (Proceedings in other Jurisdictions) Act 1975 of the United Kingdom (which was under consideration in the *State of Norway's Application* case) evolved from the Hague Convention on the Taking of Evidence Abroad in Civil or Commercial Matters 1970. Whilst both the Convention and the United Kingdom Act were intended to facilitate the provision of evidence in one jurisdiction for use in another, s. 1 of

22. At p. 8 (transcript).

the Act provides that the High Court may only make an order under it for production of the evidence sought if that evidence could have been obtained in civil proceedings conducted before the High Court. Acccordingly, bankers in England should not be vulnerable to orders under the Act as the *Tournier* principles should apply.

Much anti-disclosure legislation evolves from the desire of the government of a state to protect its interests and the interest of its nationals and is not designed principally for the protection of banks. In the United Kingdom the Protection of Trading Interests Act 1980 came about as a result of efforts by the United States Department of Justice to obtain information in anti-trust investigations (principally the sequence of *Westinghouse* cases)[23]. Basically the Act provides that a United Kingdom court shall not make an order under the Evidence (Proceedings in Other Jurisdictions) Act 1975 for giving effect to letters of request issuing out of another jurisdiction if 'it is shown' that the request infringes the jurisdiction of the United Kingdom or is otherwise prejudicial to the sovereignty of the United Kingdom. It also provides that a certificate signed by the Secretary of State to the effect that the jurisdiction of the United Kingdom would be infringed or the sovereignty of the United Kingdom would be prejudiced shall be conclusive evidence of that fact but it does leave the door open for any other methods of 'showing' such infringement or prejudice. The Act has been supported by the Protection of Trading Interests (United States Anti-Trust Measures) Order 1983 and has been followed in Australia by the Foreign Proceedings (Excessive Jurisdiction) Act 1984, a title which leaves little doubt as to the Australian view of the incursive effect of United States court orders. However, it is fair to say that Australia is one of the few states with which the United States has concluded an agreement which hints at international co-operation on disclosure (Landmark Agreement of 29 June 1982 between Australia and the United States on anti-trust laws). This is not a treaty, and therefore is not binding on either government but is regarded as an 'inter-governmental arrangement' which each government will expect the other to honour. It provides for co-operation between the two states if either state is conducting an anti-trust investigation including the provision of information which would otherwise be confidential provided that such information may not be used in evidence in any anti-trust proceedings.

23. e.g. *In re Westinghouse Electric Corp. Uranium Contract Litigation MDL Docket No. 235 (No. 2)* [1978] AC 547.

Of more direct relevance to banking secrecy was the treaty and subsequent memorandum of understanding between the United States and Switzerland (Treaty Between the USA and the Swiss Confederation on Mutual Assistance in Criminal Matters (1977) and Memorandum of Understanding, dated 31 August 1982[24]).) Under the 1977 treaty each state agreed to assist the other in the investigation of offences which were crimes in both jurisdictions. At the time of the treaty, and indeed the memorandum of understanding, insider trading was not a criminal offence under Swiss law and as a result the 1977 treaty was of no assistance to the Securities and Exchange Commission (SEC) in halting the rising tide of securities law violations in the United States. However, the memorandum assured the United States of Swiss co-operation in the investigation of insider trading offences despite the absence of criminal sanctions in Switzerland and, in particular, provided a mechanism for the SEC to obtain details of parties suspected of carrying on illegal securities transactions and records of their banking transactions.

CONCLUSIONS

No state will willingly accept an invasion of its sovereignty. Some states have paid lip service to the notion that comity should permit another state limited access to information held by bankers which would otherwise not be available due to the first state's banking secrecy law, but the reality is that all states which recognise the duty of confidentiality are loathe to allow the duty to be breached at the behest of a foreigner. Recognising that they cannot, on the one hand, defend their national status quo and, on the other, expect to have instant access to information the disclosure of which would be contrary to the law of other states, most states, with the exception of the United States, have not attempted to impose their own requirements in other jurisdictions.

But that is not good enough. However irritating the incursion of United States disclosure orders into the sanctity of other jurisdictions may have been, the aggression and persistence of United States government agencies in attempting to trace the proceeds of crime are to be applauded. There are categories of crime like drug offences, fraud and theft which are offences in all jurisdictions and it is in the interest of all states that information concerning them should be freely available. Some believe that only an international convention

24. 12 *International Legal Materials*, 916 (1973); 15 *ibid*. 283 (1976); 22 *ibid*. 1 (1983).

can provide a workable solution, but presumably a network of bilateral agreements would work as well, in the same way as double tax treaties have proved generally effective. However, either course will take time and criminals will not wait. There are two other, speedier, solutions which could be adopted in the United Kingdom:

(a) Banks could introduce standard conditions (or amend their existing standard conditions) to give them the right to respond to an order from a foreign court.

(b) Parliament could pass a short Act abolishing the duty of confidentiality altogether. At least banks would be pleased to have the burden of observing the duty lifted from them.

Presumably the major objection to either of the above two courses would be the fear of the flight of capital. However, does the United Kingdom really want to retain capital that cannot afford to see the light of day?

REMEDIES AFFECTING BANK DEPOSITS

Campbell McLachlan

Introduction

The development and widespread use in England over recent years of interim court orders freezing assets before trial has created a number of novel problems for banks. Amongst the most difficult of such problems are those concerning the trans-national effect of interim orders. While the English courts have, for practical and commercial reasons, shown a persistent tendency to localise the business of banking and the responsibilities of banks, banks have not remained immune from equally strong practical and commercial pressures which have encouraged the courts to look beyond national borders in seeking to ensure that the ultimate efficacy of judgments will not be frustrated by the new opportunities presented by modern banking practices to defendants bent on avoiding adverse litigation.

The present paper focuses primarily on the Mareva injunction. First, it examines the position of banks generally, where such an injunction has been granted. Secondly, the often contradictory course which the courts have followed in resolving whether such an injunction may be granted in relation to foreign assets will be charted. Thirdly, the implications for banks of recent decisions on extra-territorial Marevas will be discussed. Then the particular rules relating to the grant of injunctions in support of proprietary tracing claims will be examined. Finally, as a policy matter, some suggestions will be offered as to the proper ambit and role of the jurisdiction to grant interim relief. However, it may be useful to begin by recalling the genesis and basic elements of the Mareva injunction.

THE MAREVA INJUNCTION

The Mareva injunction has become such a common tool in civil litigation, that it is difficult to imagine life without it. Yet, until 1975, the rule had been that 'you cannot get an injunction to restrain a man who is alleged to be a debtor from parting with his property'[1]. The bar on pre-trial freezing of assets was a derogation from the general equitable jurisdiction to grant interim injunctions. Further, common law systems stood alone in refusing to grant this type of relief, which had always been available in civil law countries.

The decision of Lord Denning in *Mareva Compania Naviera SA* v *International Bulk Carriers SA*[2] has ushered in over a dozen years of intensive judicial development. The original focus for the grant of such injunctions had been to prevent foreign defendants, who might have only very few assets in England, from removing those assets and thus avoiding altogether the effects of an adverse English judgment. However, the grounds for the granting of such an injunction have broadened considerably since 1975. Power to grant such injunctions received the imprimatur of Parliament by s. 37(3) of the Supreme Court Act 1981, which referred to the granting of injunctions to restrain parties, whether English or foreign, from removing their assets from the jurisdiction or otherwise dealing with them.

Three main conditions have been the basis for the grant of a Mareva[3]. These requirements are:

(a) that the plaintiff has a cause of action in England;
(b) that the plaintiff has a good arguable case on that cause of action; and
(c) that there is a real risk that the defendant will remove his assets from, or dissipate them within, the jurisdiction.

In the light of recent developments, even this formulation is too narrow. In the first place, condition (a) does not now apply, where a Mareva injunction is sought in aid of proceedings in another state party to the Brussels Convention. While an injunction may not be granted in support of foreign proceedings or arbitrations outside Brussels Convention states without the existence of an English cause of action, following the decision of the House of Lords in *The Siskina*[4], s. 25 of the Civil Jurisdiction and Judgments Act 1982 (CJJA) provides that English courts may grant interim relief for proceedings commenced in other Brussels Convention states[5]. As

1. *Robinson* v *Pickering* (1881) 16 ChD 660, 661, (CA), per James LJ.
2. [1975] 2 Lloyd's Rep 509.
3. *Ninemia* v *Trave 'The Niedersachsen'* [1984] 1 All ER 398 (CA).
4. [1979] AC 210.
5. See further, McLachlan, CA *Transnational Applications of Mareva Injunctions and Anton Piller Orders* (1987) 36 ICLQ 669 and Collins, LA *Provisional Measures, the Conflict of Laws and the Brussels Convention* (1981) 1 Y B Eur L 249.

will be seen, recent cases applying Mareva injunctions to foreign assets necessitate a qualification to condition (c).

What is the effect of such an injunction once granted? In common with injunctions generally and, indeed, much of equitable relief, the Mareva injunction operates *in personam*. This means that it does not operate directly against the property named in the injunction, as would the arrest of a ship. Nor does it give a plaintiff any security for his judgment debt.

It simply imposes a personal obligation on the defendant not to deal with certain property. The general effect on third parties is thus in line with the sanctions imposed for breach of *in personam* orders. Namely, if a third party has notice of such an order, he will be in contempt of court for committing acts contrary to it[6].

The effect on banks

It was concern over the possible consequences in contempt, and a general desire to clarify their position as the class of third parties most commonly affected by Mareva injunctions, which led the major trading banks to apply to the Court of Appeal in *Z Ltd v A-Z and AA-LL*[7]. The Court of Appeal affirmed the basic principle that a bank which acted contrary to such an injunction, and with knowledge of its existence, would be guilty of contempt. The existence of the injunction provides a defence for the bank in refusing to pay monies out of the defendant's bank account. The bank, along with other third parties affected by the injunction, is to be indemnified by the plaintiff for all costs reasonably incurred in complying with it. Kerr LJ stressed the importance of drafting the injunction as precisely as possible to confine its effect to stated sums, and, if possible, to assist the banks by naming relevant bank branches and accounts.

The definition of what acts or omissions would constitute contempt in the case of banks presents difficult problems. Eveleigh LJ stressed the necessity for some form of *mens rea*. An innocent third party could only be guilty of contempt if he knowingly acted contrary to the terms of the court's order. He may, however, have gone too far in requiring actual knowledge of the injunction on the part of the servant of the bank committing the relevant breach. Arlidge and

6. *Seaward* v *Paterson* (1897) 1 Ch 545 and *Ackro (Automation) Ltd* v *Rex Chainbelt Inc* [1971] 1 WLR 1676.
7. [1982] 1 QB 558.

Eady[8] argue that a reckless failure to take the necessary steps to prevent a breach may be sufficient.

Two aspects of the bank's position when one of its customers is subject to a Mareva injunction, deserve a special mention. The first is the position of the bank itself as creditor of the defendant. The position of a normal trade creditor is that, if the injunction covers all the defendant's funds or enough of those funds to render payment to the creditor impossible, he must apply to the court for a variation of the order[9]. Following such an application, the court may grant what has become known as an Angel Bell order allowing the defendant to pay his ordinary trade creditors. Banks are, however, in a privileged position in this respect. Since *Oceanica* v *Mineralimportexport*[10] it has been common practice to include a clause in Mareva orders preserving a bank's right of set off against its customer. As Lloyd J made clear in that case, without such a clause the bank would be in the same position as other creditors and would have to apply to the court for a variation.

The position of banks in relation to letters of credit, performance bonds and bank guarantees also merits elucidation. The purpose of the majority of documentary credits is to protect persons contracting with the bank's customer by means of an independent obligation entered into by the bank: *Siporex Trade SA* v *Banque Indosuez*[11]. Indeed, they have been described as the 'life blood of commerce'.[12] Thus, if the defendant defaults on his obligations to a third party and the bank is thereby required to pay out under the letter of credit or performance bond, it must perform that obligation regardless of any Mareva injunction because the obligation is that of the bank. In the normal case, it would have a right of recourse against the defendant which it might satisfy by means of its right of set off. In the reverse situation of the defendant receiving funds under a bank guarantee or other documentary credit, *The Bhoja Trader* is authority for the proposition that a Mareva injunction will not issue to prevent a defendant from receiving funds due to him under such an instrument, although the injunction may cover funds once they are in the defendant's hands.

---

8. *The Law of Contempt* 1982, 68.
9. *Iraqi Ministry of Defence* v *Arcepey Shipping Co. 'The Angel Bell'* [1981] 1 QB 65.
10. [1983] 1 WLR 1294.
11. [1986] 2 Lloyd's Rep 146.
12. Per Donaldson LJ, *Intraco Ltd* v *Notis Shipping Corp, 'The Bhoja Trader'* [1981] 2 Lloyd's Rep 256.

EXTRATERRITORIAL APPLICATION

Equity has not shrunk, in granting other types of injunction, from ordering those over whom it has *in personam* jurisdiction to do or refrain from doing acts abroad[13]. Although in doing this, the English courts have always stressed that they are only imposing personal obligations on a person subject to their jurisdiction, it is of course the case that such orders can and do have effects (sometimes unanticipated by the English courts) elsewhere. As Dr Mann has pointed out[14]:

'The mere fact that a state's judicial or administrative agencies are internationally entitled to subject a person to their personal or "curial" jurisdiction does not by any means permit them to regulate by their orders such person's conduct abroad. This they may do only if the state of the forum also has substantive jurisdiction to regulate conduct in the manner defined in the order.'

In contrast to the position with regard to injunctions generally, and perhaps as a consequence of the mischief for which the Mareva injunction was originally developed, it has until recently been thought that such injunctions could not be granted in relation to foreign assets. They were to prevent the removal from England (or the dissipation within England) of the defendant's assets.

Initially established by *The Bhoja Trader*, this was authoritively affirmed by the Court of Appeal in *Ashtiani* v *Kashi*[15]. The case illustrates the close nexus between the Mareva injunction, its use to obtain ancillary orders for discovery of the defendant's assets, and the obtaining of foreign pre-trial orders, in the context of increasingly multi-jurisdictional litigation.

In *Ashtiani*, the parties were all Iranian citizens. The plaintiffs were resident in Iran, the defendants in England. The background to the parties' dispute involved a business venture for the transportation of grain from the United States to Iran, and damages awarded by a United States court for fraud committed by a trading partner of that business venture. The plaintiffs sought the recovery of money allegedly owed to them by the defendant under the terms of a

---

13. *Kerr on Injunctions* (6th ed., 1927), 11.
14. In *The Doctrine of Jurisdiction in International Law* (1964) 111 Hague Receuil 146, cited with approval by Hoffmann J in *Mackinnon* v *Donaldson* [1986] 2 WLR 453, 9.
15. [1987] QB 888.

compromise agreement for division of the sum of damages. In connection with this action, the plaintiffs sought and obtained a wide ranging Mareva injunction over the defendant's assets in England, together with an ancillary order for discovery of 'the full value of its assets within and without the jurisdiction'.

Such an order for discovery of assets outside the jurisdiction had been granted in a number of previous English cases: *CBS UK Ltd* v *Lambert*[16]; *PCW* (*Underwriting Agencies*) *Limited* v *Dixon*[17]; *Bayer* v *Winter* (No 3.)[18]. In the latter case, Hoffman J had observed (362) that, if the defendant's assets presently within the jurisdiction were insufficient to meet the plantiff's claim, it would be a 'pointless insularity' for an English court not to grant a discovery order to enable a plaintiff to obtain interim relief in foreign courts.

In *Ashtiani*, the order had revealed substantial assets in bank accounts in Guernsey, Belgium and Luxembourg. Acting on this information, the plaintiffs obtained freezing orders in those jurisdictions. The defendant then went back to court to argue that such an order should never have been made by an English court in the first place. The Court of Appeal agreed. Dillon LJ found that a discovery order made in support of a Mareva injunction should, except in special circumstances, only extend to the same territorial limits as the Mareva injunction itself. Relying on the language of s. 37, SCA 1981, Dillon LJ found that, although sub-section (1) did not restrict the court's jurisdiction to grant such an injunction over foreign assets, sub-section (3) did reflect the general practice of applying a Mareva to English assets only.

He raised four reasons of principle for this limitation:

(i) that it could be oppressive to the defendant to have his assets in many other parts of the world frozen;

(ii) that it was difficult for the English court to control or police enforcement proceedings in other jurisdictions;

(iii) that an order for discovery involved the invasion of an otherwise absolute right to privacy;

(iv) that foreign attachment orders might do precisely what the Mareva injunction was designed not to do, namely give the plaintiff security over the defendant's property.

While *Ashtiani* appeared to put the matter beyond doubt in England,

16. [1983] Ch 37.
17. [1983] 2 All ER 158.
18. [1986] FSR 357.

developments in other parts of the common law world were questioning such a narrowly confined approach. In the New South Wales case of *Ballabil Holdings* v *Hospital Products*[19], a New South Wales company had removed its assets from the jurisdiction in the 24 hours between the commencement of proceedings and the grant of a Mareva injunction. The court upheld the injunction over those assets. A particularly important factor weighing with the court in that case seems to have been the deliberate evasion of the court's process by removal of assets from the jurisdiction. *Ballabil* was followed in South Australia by *Coombs and Barei* v *Dynasty*[20]. However, Millhouse J was clearly influenced by the fact that the defendant's assets were in other states and territories of Australia, and that it would be 'absurd' to allow a defendant to avoid a Mareva injunction by locating his assets in another state of the Commonwealth. In a third case, *Yandil Holdings* v *Insurance Co. of North America*[21], Rogers J had the opportunity to consider whether *Ashtiani*'s case affected these Australian developments. He found that there were 'special circumstances' which justified an order for discovery of foreign assets.

The Hong Kong High Court was prepared to depart further from *Ashtiani* in *Asean Resources* v *Ka Wah International*[22]. Sears J found that he did have jurisdiction to grant a Mareva injunction over foreign assets. In that case, the company in question was a Hong Kong company, but its only unencumbered assets were shares in a Singapore company. The share certificates were deposited with Hong Kong solicitors. Sears J found it particularly relevant that these assets were specifically identifiable, held in Hong Kong and owned by a company clearly subject to the personal jurisdiction of the Hong Kong courts.

Meanwhile, in England, the Court of Appeal reaffirmed *Ashtiani* in *Reilly* v *Fryer*[23]. That was another discovery case, where, as an aid to execution after judgment, the plaintiffs had sought discovery of all of the defendant's assets outside the jurisdiction together with a Mareva injunction over his assets within the jurisdiction. The worldwide discovery order was refused. Counsel had not sought to distinguish *Ashtiani* and, on the facts, the extent of the defendant's assets within the jurisdiction had not yet been conclusively deter-

19. [1985] 1 NSWLR 155.
20. (1986) 42 SASR 413.
21. [1987] 7 NSWLR 571.
22. [1987] LRC (Comm) 835.
23. *Financial Times*, 6 May 1988.

mined. However, discovery in aid of a post-judgment Mareva injunction was now in a somewhat anomalous position compared to the general right to disclosure of assets after judgment established by *Interpool Ltd* v *Gallani*[24] and *Maclaine Watson* v *International Tin Council (No. 2)*.[25]

Within a matter of weeks, the Court of Appeal had the opportunity to reconsider the grant of Mareva injunctions over foreign assets in *Babanaft* v *Bassatne*[26]. *Babanaft* was also concerned with the grant of a Mareva injunction after judgment. Despite the helpful dicta of Sir John Donaldson MR in *DST* v *Rakoil*[27] that a post-judgment injunction was not properly characterisable as a Mareva injunction because the plaintiff had already obtained judgment, and thus had a subsisting judgment debt for the enforcement of which he was entitled to the assistance of the court, and should not have to meet the conditions imposed on the grant of a Mareva injunction, the Mareva seems to hold such pervasive appeal that the terminology has persisted in post-judgment cases. This is unfortunate, since the policy considerations and consequent legal requirements may well be different in each case. Nevertheless, the judgments of the Court of Appeal in *Babanaft* contain much of relevance to the pre-trial situation.

The factual context before the court in *Babanaft* was that the plaintiff company had obtained judgment against the defendant brothers for over US$15 million. The Bassatnes were found to be carrying on business from a variety of locations and through a range of companies established in well-known tax havens. Having obtained an order from Vinelott J, the plaintiff proceeded to notify some 47 entities in various countries, including banks where the Bassatne brothers had accounts.

Kerr, Neill and Nicholls LJJ each delivered separate judgments and, in so doing, explored some novel approaches to extraterritorial Marevas. Neill and Nicholls LJJ were both members of the court which had decided *Ashtiani*. Neill LJ commented that *Ashtiani* had accurately reflected the way in which the jurisdiction to grant Mareva injunctions had developed up to that point, but that the court did have jurisdiction to grant a Mareva injunction over foreign assets. He accepted that the law might well develop beyond the point reached

24. [1987] 3 WLR 1042.
25. [1987] 1 WLR 1711, at 1717 per Millett J, affirmed, (CA), *The Times*, 5 May 1988.
26. *The Independent*, 30 June 1988.
27. [1987] 3 WLR 1023, 1036.

in *Ashtiani*. In any event, *Babanaft* was a different case because it concerned a post-judgment order. Once the plaintiff had obtained judgment, Neill LJ thought that an injunction could be granted quite commonly over all of the defendant's assets whether within or without the jurisdiction. In order to stress the *in personam* character of the order, Neill LJ suggested that a proviso expressly excluding any obligation on third parties be added. He said little about pre-trial relief, preferring to leave a decision on this to a later case.

Nicholls LJ pointed out that *Ashtiani* was a disclosure case where the court had been troubled about the unsatisfactory, even oppressive, consequences that might befall a defendant if he were compelled by an English court to disclose the whereabouts of his overseas assets in advance of judgment. After judgment the position was different because English law enabled a judgment creditor to attach assets of the judgment debtor. The existence of a judgment justified the grant of an injunction and of associated disclosure orders in order to ensure its efficacy. He also found it to be wrong and unacceptable that such an order should bind third parties in their actions outside the jurisdiction.

Kerr LJ, although he assented to a form of order expressly limited to the defendants personally, delivered a judgment preferring a further variation of this, namely, that the order should not affect third parties unless and to the extent that, it had been enforced by the courts of the state in which the assets were located. Describing this as an international approach, he held that the same considerations were applicable in pre-trial cases. He rested this alternative formulation on an interpretation of Art. 24 of the Brussels Convention. Although the primary effect of Art. 24 had been to allow the court of one contracting state to grant interim measures in support of proceedings in another state (as discussed above), Kerr LJ found that its secondary effect had been to make interim orders made in one state enforceable in another. This possibility, discussed by Collins in the European Year Book[28] could be derived from the decisions of the European Court in *De Cavel* v *De Cavel (No. 1)*[29] and *Denilauler* v *Couchet Frères*[30]. If, reasoned Kerr LJ, an English Mareva injunction might become enforceable under the Brussels Convention in other European states, then clearly it was not contrary to international comity to make such orders over foreign assets.

28. Op. cit.
29. [1979] ECR 1055.
30. [1980] ECR 1553.

One month after *Babanaft*, a differently constituted Court of Appeal[31] took another look at the extraterritorial Mareva in the remarkable case of *Republic of Haiti v Duvalier*[32]. In that case, the Republic of Haiti was proceeding against its former president, Jean-Claude 'Baby Doc' Duvalier and family for recovery of sums in excess of US$120 million, said to have been embezzled from the Republic while Mr Duvalier was in office. There was evidence that the Duvaliers, now resident in France, were engaging in an elaborate scheme to take their assets beyond the reach of courts of law. The Republic had brought proceedings in France and then sought a Mareva injunction and ancillary orders for discovery in England. The case thus involved the grant of an injunction in support of proceedings in another state party to the Brussels Convention under s. 25, CJJA 1982. In order to give full effect to this section, Staughton LJ found that service of a writ for such injunctive relief could be effected under RSC Ord. 11, rule 1(2) without leave. The court then went on to consider whether such an injunction could apply to foreign assets. Although the point had been conceded by counsel, Staughton LJ considered the recent authorities and held that:

'. . . There is jurisdiction to grant a Mareva injunction, pending trial, for assets worldwide; and that cases where it will be appropriate to grant such an injunction will be rare—if not very rare indeed.'

Nevertheless, counsel had sought to argue that, in the exercise of its discretion, the court should refuse to grant a Mareva over foreign assets in the circumstances of the case. Counsel had observed that the English courts had no jurisdiction on the merits, that none of the defendants were resident in England, that there was no judgment against them, that the assets concerned were mainly, if not wholly, outside the jurisdiction, and that the proper court to make such an order was either the court having jurisdiction on the merits, or the courts having jurisdiction where the assets were located. Staughton LJ swept these objections aside. What weighed most persuasively with him was that the defendants were trying to conceal their assets and avoid judgment and that it was likely that information could be obtained on discovery in England which would significantly assist in locating the assets.

Finally, the '*Babanaft* proviso' on the position of third parties was

31. Staughton, Stocker and Fox LJJ.
32. *The Times*, 28 July 1988.

considered. Staughton LJ accepted that there should be such a proviso. He preferred the formulation offered by Kerr LJ because:

'... it may encourage the courts of other countries to enforce the English order; and if it has that effect it is in my opinion desirable.'

Finally, he held that the proviso should only apply to assets outside England and Wales, and to acts done outside England and Wales, and that it should not (in contrast to the approach taken by Nicholls LJ in *Babanaft*) apply to individuals resident in England and Wales, because:

'... I would find it offensive that [an English resident] should be free to cross the channel and sign away the money.'

A further clarification was handed down by the Court of Appeal in *Derby and Co. Ltd v Weldon*[33]. The claim was once again for a substantial sum, some £34 million. The defendants had been directors of the plaintiffs, and it was alleged that they had made wrongful profits at the plaintiffs' expense.

Nicholls LJ acknowledged that court had jurisdiction to make Mareva injunctions and associated discovery orders both before and after judgment:

'The jurisdiction is established, but what is still being worked out, in this fast developing area of law, is that manner in which, in practice, the court should exercise its discret..onary power under this wide jurisdiction.'

The court approved the Kerr formulation of the '*Babanaft* proviso'. At counsel's suggestion, it added a further proviso, namely, that the plaintiffs should give an undertaking that any application to a foreign court to enforce the order would not be made without first obtaining leave from the English court. This would give the English court an opportunity to consider whether, in the case of the particular foreign order sought to be obtained, the result might be oppressive to the defendant and, generally, to co-ordinate the litigation. The court rejected suggestions made by counsel that previous cases supported the proposition that a world-wide order could only be made where there was some proof of dishonesty on the part of the defendants.

---

33. May, Parker and Nicholls LJJ, *The Times*, 2 August 1988. See also *Derby and Co. Ltd v Weldon (No. 3)*, *The Independent*, 17 November 1988.

Each case had to depend on its own facts, although it was still accepted that the situation must be 'appropriately grave before it will be just and convenient for such a Draconian order to be made'[34].

Extraterritoriality and banks

Thus, within a few short months, and at the expense (as Parker LJ pointed out in *Derby* v *Weldon*) of an inordinate amount of Court of Appeal time, the law on the extraterritorial effect of Mareva injunctions has been reversed. In *Ashtiani*, the Court of Appeal had accepted that there might well be jurisdiction to grant such orders over foreign assets, but had set its face firmly against allowing such orders in the exercise of discretion. The court, in *Babanaft*, *Duvalier*, and *Derby* v *Weldon* was undoubtedly presented with a series of extraordinary cases, all allegedly involving misuse of funds on a very large scale by defendants using the full resources of the modern transnational finance system. They were, as Kerr LJ pointed out in *Babanaft*, situations which 'cry out ... as a matter of justice to plaintiffs ... for disclosure orders and Mareva-type injunctions covering foreign assets'. Nevertheless, the judges were clearly troubled by this new leap into extraterritorial realms. In part, their concern was that the order should not operate oppressively against defendants, but they were more particularly concerned with oppressive effects against third parties, especially banks. Correspondence sent out by the plaintiffs' solicitors in *Babanaft* to foreign banks had warned them of the possible sanction of contempt, and had pointed out that contempt proceedings could be brought against bank officers at English branches. There had in some cases been indignant responses from the foreign banks.

Banks can be placed in very awkward situations indeed where their duty to their customer to pay out sums in the customer's account is brought into conflict with a mandatory direction of foreign law. This is particularly acute where the bank would, by honouring obligations to the customer, expose itself or its officers to criminal prosecution[35]. However, even without the protection of the '*Babanaft*

---

34. Per Nicholls LJ.
35. Compare with the recent case involving the application of the United States Libyan Sanctions Regulations to United States banks in London: *Libyan Arab Foreign Bank* v *Bankers Trust Co.* [1988] 1 Lloyd's Rep 259.

proviso', it is submitted that a foreign bank would not be bound under English law to comply with a Mareva injunction over assets outside England, and that its officers, whether resident in England or not, would not be liable in contempt proceedings for failure to comply with the order.

This conclusion stems from a consideration of the territorial restrictions on contempt. The proceeding for civil contempt is criminal or quasi criminal: *Re Bramblevale*; *Comet Products (UK)* v *Hawkex Plastics Ltd*[36]. It is well established that the criminal law is strictly territorial in operation unless statute expressly provides otherwise: *Treacy* v *DPP*; *DPP* v *Stonehouse*[37]. As Lord Keith explained in the latter case (90):

'... the general principle of the territoriality of crime is of great importance. The English courts do not assert jurisdiction to try any person whether a citizen of this country or not, for acts done in a foreign land. The more correct approach is to say that such an act cannot in principle constitute a crime by the law of England ... In the field of statutory offences, there is a strong presumption that Parliament has not legislated so as to attribute criminal consequences here to acts done abroad.'

Thus, an official in a foreign bank outside England, who fails to ensure that the English Mareva injunction is given effect should not be subject to criminal liability in England. The English branch of a foreign bank will only have responsibility over assets held by it in England. The courts have been reluctant to impose responsibilities on foreign banks for their acts abroad, simply because they have branches in England: *R* v *Grossman*; *Mackinnon* v *Donaldson Lufkin and Jenrette Securities*[38]. Thus, unless an official of the bank in England commits acts in England which contribute to the breach of the injunction, it is unlikely that any contempt of proceedings could be brought against the English branch.

Banks which might have been unwilling to take such a robust approach will be encouraged by the '*Babanaft* proviso'. As a result of the three Court of Appeal decisions, it now seems that an express

---

36. [1970] Ch 128. [1971] 2 QB 97; but cf. *Garvin* v *Domus Publishing Ltd* [1988] 3 WLR 344, where Walton J suggested that the criminal aspects of civil contempt proceedings and the sanction of imprisonment did not affect their status as for the enforcement of civil rights.
37. [1971] AC 537 (HL). [1978] AC 55 (HL).
38. (1981) 73 Cr App R 302. [1986] Ch 482.

exclusion of third party liability will become a standard requirement in drafting extraterritorial Mareva orders. Nevertheless, banks should be aware that their customer will continue to be personally subject to the Mareva injunction, and will be breaking its terms by removing funds from a foreign bank account. Moreover, as Nicholls LJ noted in *Derby* v *Weldon*, the qualification to the '*Babanaft* proviso' added by Staughton LJ in *Duvalier* to the effect that natural persons resident in England should continue to be bound by the injunction even in respect of acts done abroad, may not be entirely satisfactory. It remains for a future case to chart the responsibilities of London branches of foreign banks and their officials in relation to funds held abroad, a point which clearly troubled both Nicholls LJ in *Babanaft* and Staughton LJ in *Duvalier*.

INJUNCTIONS, TRACING AND PROPRIETARY CLAIMS

Does the fact that the relief sought by the plaintiff is the return or tracing of property, rather than merely damages for a personal claim, affect the availability of injunctive relief over foreign assets or the position of banks? The distinction between proprietary and personal claims in the law relating to pretrial injunctions goes back at least as far as *Lister & Co.* v *Stubbs*[39]. That case had been one of the primary authorities for the proposition that a Mareva type injunction was not available before judgment because[40]:

> '... We should be simply ordering the defendant to pay into court a sum of money in his possession because there is a prima facie case against him that at the hearing it will be established that he owes money to the plaintiffs.'

In that case, Stubbs, a foreman of Lister & Co., had allegedly entered into a corrupt bargain with one of Lister's suppliers. The company sought restitution of the money. It was held that they were not entitled to follow the money and that there was no trust in their favour over it. All that Lister & Co. could enforce was Stubb's liability to account for the money. It was acknowledged, however, that, had there been a right to follow the money, an injunction would have been available to restrain the defendant from dealing with it.

Where the plaintiff does indeed assert that money which is either

39. (1890) 45 Ch 1.
40. At 14, per Cotton LJ.

in the hands of the defendant or has passed through his hands belongs to the plaintiff, the courts will not shrink from ordering its return, whether or not property is currently situate in England. A recent case in point is *Guinness* v *Saunders and Ward*[41]. It was held that Mr Ward was constructive trustee of some £5.2 million received by him from the company and that he was liable to repay it. The fact that the money was no longer in England was irrelevant.

Will an injunction issue over foreign assets in support of a proprietary tracing claim? Even in *Ashtiani*, Dillon LJ had accepted that 'obviously' a Mareva injunction could extend to foreign assets where the title for those assets was in question. Both *Haiti* v *Duvalier* and *Derby* v *Weldon* were potentially proprietary or tracing claims. Staughton LJ usefully discussed whether there was any distinction to be drawn between proprietary and personal claims in *Duvalier*:

'It may be that the powers of the court are wider, and certainly discretion is more readily exercised, if a plaintiff's claim is what is called a tracing claim. For my part, I think that the true distinction lies between a proprietary claim on the one hand, and a claim which seeks only a money judgment on the other. A proprietory claim is one by which the plaintiff seeks the return of chattels or land which are his property, or claims that a specified debt is owed by a third party to him and not the defendant.

Thus far, there is no difficulty. A plaintiff who seeks to enforce a claim of that kind will all the more readily be afforded interim remedies in order to preserve the asset which he is seeking to recover, than one who merely seeks a judgment for debt or damages. But if the asset has been converted into some other form of property, the question of tracing arises.... [I]f the defendant misappropriated the plaintiff's credit balance with the X bank, and established a credit with the Y bank from the proceeds, the plaintiff claims that the debt due from the Y bank is his property. In that last case, if the proceedings are brought by the plaintiff against the defendant only, the relief claimed can be no more than a declaration, and an injunction against interference with the plaintiff's property. Ultimately, the right must be enforced against the debtor—in my example, the Y bank.'

He held that, in the instant case, it was as yet unclear whether the French proceedings were in the nature of a proprietary claim or not.

41. Browne-Wilkinson V-C, *The Independent*, 16 April 1987; (CA) [1988] 1 WLR 863.

He thus proceeded to consider the availability of injunctive relief over foreign assets generally. Whether the claim was properly classifiable as a proprietary or personal one was also an issue, but not decided at the interlocutory stage, in *Derby* v *Weldon*.

While the matter is thus still somewhat obscure, proprietary claims raise important, but conflicting, policy considerations. On the one hand, the money belongs to the plaintiff, and so the court should be readier to assist in its recovery. Remedies such as RSC Ord. 29, rule 2 exist to preserve specific property which is the subject of a proprietary claim. On the other hand, a proprietary order over foreign property is more likely to be characterised as a breach of international jurisdiction[42]. The fact that relief is given by way of injunction over someone subject to the personal jurisdiction of the court may not be sufficient to cure this objection. In any event, if the claim is genuinely a proprietary one, it will usually be necessary to institute proceedings in the country where the property is.

In *Chase Manhattan Bank* v *Israel–British Bank*[43], Goulding J was confronted with an action to trace and recover in equity sums paid to the defendant bank in error by the plaintiff, a New York bank. The action was necessitated by the insolvency of the defendant bank. Goulding J's decision raised, but did not resolve, the difficult issue as to which law should be applied to determine the existence and nature of the right to trace. He found that, fortunately, there was no material difference between New York and English law on tracing. Potentially, he would have had to resolve both the proper law of the obligation to return the property and whether the remedy of tracing was to be characterised as procedural or substantive.

Money was also sought to be recovered, where the alleged cause of action had arisen in a foreign country, in the Irish case of *Larkins* v *National Union of Mineworkers and Bank of Ireland Finance Ltd*[44]. In that case, Larkins and others had been appointed as sequestrators of the assets of the National Union of Mineworkers and sought to recover assets of the union held with the second defendant. In separate English proceedings, the existing trustees of the union's assets were removed and a receiver appointed. Mareva type injunctions were sought in Ireland to preserve the assets. Barrington J dismissed the claims of the sequestrators on the grounds that the sequestration

---

42. See, for example, Dr F A Mann's critique of *US* v *First National City Bank*, 379 US 378 (1965) in *The Doctrine of International Jurisdiction Revisited After Twenty Years* (1984) 186 Hague Receuil 13, 52–3.

43. [1981] 1 Ch 105.

44. [1985] IR 671.

process was penal in effect and the Irish High Court would not entertain a suit brought for the purpose of enforcing a foreign state's penal law. However, the receiver's claim was found to be good and, under the circumstances, an injunction was granted to preserve the Irish funds until permanent trustees of the union's property could be identified or appointed in accordance with the provisions of English law. Barrington J was also prepared to order inspection of the bank's books in order to ensure that the funds were still held with it.

This paper has not sought to deal with a bank's obligations to disclose information. However, it should be pointed out that, in tracing claims, it is very likely that the bank will be joined as a party to litigation in order to obtain discovery under the principle in *Norwich Pharmacal* v *Customs and Excise*[45] that a person who gets mixed up in another's wrongdoing has a duty to assist the person who has been wronged by giving him information. This principle has found new life in the context of discovery orders in support of Mareva injunctions in tracing claims following the cases of *A* v *C* and *Bankers Trust Co* v *Shapira*[46]. In each case, fraud was alleged, and the bank where it was said the proceeds of the fraud were held was joined as a defendant along with the fraudsters. Lord Denning MR explained the new principle in *Bankers Trust* in the following terms:

'This new jurisdiction must, of course, be carefully exercised. It is a strong thing to order a bank to disclose the state of its customer's account and the documents and correspondence relating to it. It should only be done where there is a good ground for thinking the money in the bank is the plaintiff's money—as, for instance, when the customer has got the money by fraud, or other wrong-doing—and paid it into his account at the bank. The plaintiff who has been defrauded has a right in equity to follow the money. He is entitled, in Lord Atkin's words, to lift the latch of the banker's door: see *Banque Belge pour l'Etranger* v *Hambrouck* [1921] 1 KB 321, 355. ... If the plaintiff's equity is to be of any avail, he must be given access to the bank's books and documents—for that is the only way of tracing the money or knowing what has happened to it. ... So the court, in order to give effect to equity, will be prepared in a proper case to make an order on the bank for their discovery.'

45. [1974] AC 133.
46. [1980] 2 All ER 347. [1980] 1 WLR 1274.

He then went on to impose the usual safeguards of a plaintiff's undertaking to reimburse the bank for the expenses of compliance and an undertaking not to use the information gained for any other purpose.

Could such an order extend to compel an English branch to produce documents held by other branches or its head office abroad? Templeman J was prepared to so order in *London and Counties Securities* v *Caplan*[47]. However, in *Mackinnon* v *Donaldson Lufkin and Jenrette Securities*[48], Hoffmann J was not prepared to extend this duty to disclose to an order requiring London branch of the defendant's bank, Citibank, to produce documents held in its New York offices, for the purposes of an English fraud action. He said of *Caplan* that 'the infringement of sovereignty was excused by a commercial equivalent of hot pursuit' (at 498). He proceeded to hold that a *Norwich Pharmacal* order's 'international jurisdictional limits are the same as those of a subpoena *duces tecum* or an order under the Bankers' Books Evidence Act 1879' (at 499), namely, limited to documents held in England.

CONCLUSION

The cases discussed in this article show how far the courts have been prepared to go in using the English judicial process in order to secure assets wherever situate for the benefit of actual or potential judgment creditors. Yet the Mareva injunction imposes a heavy responsibility not merely on the defendant but also on third parties, and it will have been evident that banks bear the brunt of this responsibility.

In the fast changing world of preemptive remedies, the courts have shown themselves to be keenly aware of the way in which the limitations of territorial jurisdiction may be exploited by unscrupulous defendants. However, it may be questioned whether the attempt to avoid a pointless insularity and to replace it with an internationalist approach may not come to be seen as imperialist and, worse, ineffective. Kerr LJ in *Babanaft* sought to find some international justification for an extended Mareva jurisdiction in the Brussels Convention. However, it is submitted that such a justification fails on two counts.

First, the Brussels Convention is not an example of international unification. It is rather, in common with much European community

47. Unreported, 26 May 1978.
48. [1986] Ch 482.

law, a product of European protectionism. In a number of respects it places non-member states in a worse position than that which they might have encountered pre-Convention[49]. The Convention cannot thus be regarded as an indication of an internationally acceptable approach.

In relation to interim orders, s. 25, CJJA 1982 places a plaintiff in proceedings instituted in any Brussels Convention state in a better position to plaintiffs in non-member states.

However, even if the Brussels Convention is relevant to an English court's formulation of the extraterritorial extent of Mareva injunctions (which it undoubtedly is in relation to member states) it is submitted that the approach suggested by Kerr LJ as stemming from the 'secondary effect' of Art. 24 is a misconstruction of the scheme of the Convention in relation to interim measures. Although his point is supported to some extent by dicta of the European Court in *Denilauler*, the European Court did observe in the same case[50]:

> 'The courts of the place . . . where the assets subject to the measures sought are located, are those best able to assess the circumstances which may lead to the grant or refusal of the measures sought or to the laying down of procedures and conditions which the plaintiff must observe in order to guarantee the provisional and protective character of the measures ordered.'

Thus, while the Convention in most cases restricts the hearing of substantive proceedings to the courts of one member state, interim measures in support of those proceedings are to be awarded in the country where the assets are located. The excesses of the *Babanaft* approach are well illustrated by *Haiti* v *Duvalier*, where the English court was prepared both to assume jurisdiction to grant interim measures under its enlarged powers by virtue of s. 25, CJJA 1982, and to extend those measures worldwide, despite the fact that there were few if any assets in England and that a French court had conduct of the substance of the matter.

A general problem with the extraterritorial Mareva is the limitations on the court's power to enforce it. As discussed above, the normal consequences in contempt for breaches by third parties are unlikely to apply in relation to acts done abroad. The ultimate sanctions of enforcement by English court officials cannot be carried out in foreign territory. What is left, therefore, is a personal obli-

49. See notably Arts. 3 and 4.
50. [1980] ECR 1553, 1570.

41

gation on the defendant, which must be enforced as best as possible against him. If the defendant is actually present in England this may not present too many difficulties. However, if the English court takes jurisdiction over the defendant on some other ground, and he is not present, the order risks becoming an empty one.

Outside England, it is questionable whether the injunction would prevail over the defendant's obligations to his ordinary creditors.

Finally, as the old cases on injunctions acknowledge, some attempt must be made to balance the interests of foreign courts and foreign states[51].

'An English court will not pronounce a decree, even *in personam* which can have no specific operation without the intervention of a foreign court, and which ... would probably be treated as a *brutum fulmen*'.

In *Mackinnon*, Hoffman J stressed the need for some 'self imposed limitation' in relation to extraterritorial court orders[52]:

'The principle is that a state should refrain from demanding obedience to its sovereign authority by foreigners in respect of their conduct outside the jurisdiction' (at 493).

While the limitations in relation to third parties established in the recent cases go some way towards mitigating these problems, it does seem that the English courts are now launched upon an uncertain course, over territory which they have previously forborne from charting.

---

51. *Kerr on Injunctions*, at p. 11.
52. [1986] Ch 482, 493.

COURT ORDERS AFFECTING FOREIGN BANK DEPOSITS

Robert R. Pennington

Introduction

The validity and effectiveness of judgments or orders made by a court in any country in respect of an account held with a bank in the same or a different country by a person or corporation who has, or who lacks, a local connection (by reason of nationality, domicile or residence) with the country in which the court functions, depend on the rules of private international law applied in the country where it is sought to enforce the judgment or order. There are therefore at least three, and possibly four, variables to be taken into account: first, the location of the court which makes the judgment or order; secondly, the location of the bank with which the account is held (bearing in mind that the relevant location may be that of the branch of the bank at which the account was held); thirdly, the location of the customer or holder of the account; and finally, the location of the court through which it is sought to enforce the judgment or order, if it is in a different country from that of the court which made the order.

These variables will affect the application of the rules of private international law applied by the enforcing court when it comes to decide whether, under its national law, the judgment or order can be enforced by the normal processes of execution, and at an earlier stage, the variables will have affected the decision of the court which gave the judgment or made the order that it had jurisdiction to do so. If the court, which made the judgment or order, is identical with the one which is called on to enforce it, or if both courts are part of the same national system, or the same state system in federal countries, the two questions are, of course, telescoped into one. On the other hand, it may well be that the judgment or order has been made by a court of one country because by its rules of private international law the dispute falls within the jurisdiction of its courts (e.g. a dispute in respect of a contract made in, or to be performed in the country) but the judgment or order, when made, can only be effectively enforced in another country because the person against whom it was made is personally present or has assets there.

The elaboration and application of appropriate rules to determine when the courts of any country have jurisdiction to give judgments or make orders in respect of bank accounts when a foreign element is involved (e.g. because the bank or the account holder is a foreign national or resident) are usually complicated by the fact that there are no special jurisdictional rules for bank accounts. The jurisdiction of a national court is, consequently, determined by other factors relating to the matter in dispute (e.g. the place where the contract under which the account was opened was made or is to be performed). Moreover, not all disputes relating to bank accounts primarily involve the bank with which the account is held; for example, the litigation may be between a principal in country A, and his agent in country B, as to the proprietorship of a bank account opened by the agent in a third country, C, for the purpose of his agency, or as to the accountability of the agent to his principal for the credit balance on that account when it is closed by the agent. In fact, all claims to jurisdiction over a dispute which are based on the nature of the cause of action alleged, or on the place where it arose, or where the transaction giving rise to it was entered into or was to be performed, create difficulties of this kind, and it is only when the jurisdiction of a court to decide the dispute is based wholly on the personal status of the plaintiff or defendant (e.g. nationality, domicile or residence) that the question of jurisdiction concerning bank accounts is fairly simple to resolve.

Parallel difficulties arise when it is sought to enforce a judgment obtained in one country through the courts of another. Unless there is in force a treaty arrangement for the reciprocal enforcement of judgments in the two countries (as under the Foreign Judgments (Reciprocal Enforcement) Act 1933), the enforcing court can only permit its processes of execution to be used to enforce the foreign judgment by treating the judgment as itself creating a cause of action, and by deciding that that cause of action is one on which the enforcing court has jurisdiction to adjudicate under its own rules of private international law. In the remainder of this paper this last complication will be disregarded, but it is nevertheless of major practical importance. However, if the judgment is initially obtained in one of the countries which is a party to the 1968 Convention on Jurisdiction and the Enforcement of Judgments in Civil and Commercial Matters (as since amended) and it is sought to enforce the judgment in another such country, the matter is simplified by the uniformity of the jurisdictional rules contained in the Convention; if the judgment is obtained in one Convention country in conformity with those jurisdictional rules, it is automatically enforceable in all the other Convention countries[1]. In cases which do not come within the 1968 Convention (e.g. because the court whose judgment is sought to be enforced is not a court of a Convention country) the rule of English law is that: (a) the judgment will be recognised and enforced in England and Wales only if it comes within an international agreement with this country made under the Foreign Judgments (Reciprocal Enforcement Act) 1933; (b) where the judgment does not come within such an international agreement, if the person, against whom the judgment is sought to be enforced, was either the unsuccessful plaintiff in the foreign proceedings, or submitted to the jurisdiction of the foreign court by taking part in those proceedings, or by agreeing to submit to the foreign jurisdiction, or if he was resident in the country where the judgment was obtained, or if it was a company or corporation which had its centre of control and management in the foreign country at the commencement of the proceedings there.

One final introductory matter calls for mention. In determining the jurisdiction of a court to pronounce on a dispute concerning a bank account, the system of law which governs the contract between the bank and the account holder may be a relevant jurisdictional factor, either to the exclusion of all other factors (e.g. where the dispute is between the bank and the account holder), or concurrently with, or as an alternative to, other jurisdictional factors. This is a matter on which case law is well developed in all the industrially and commercially advanced countries of the world, but in this paper it will be dealt with, like the basic question of jurisdiction, only in respect of English law.

JURISDICTION

The rules applied by an English court to determine whether it has jurisdiction to entertain proceedings in respect of a bank account where a foreign element is present fall into two groups, depending on whether the foreign element relates to a country which was a party to the 1968 Convention on Jurisdiction and the Enforcement of Judgments (as since amended) or not. The countries which are

1. Convention, Art. 31(1), enacted as UK law by the Civil Jurisdiction and Judgments Act 1982, s. 2(1).

parties to that Convention comprise the nine full member states of the European Communities, but they may be enlarged in the future by other member states acceding to the Convention. If, on the one hand, the foreign element in the dispute concerns another such full member state, the jurisdiction of its courts over a dispute relating to a bank account is exhaustively defined by the Convention. If, on the other hand, the foreign element concerns any other country, such as the United States, the jurisdiction of an English court is determined by whether the writ or other originating process in the action has been served on the defendant or respondent in England and Wales, or whether it can be served on him elsewhere with leave of the court under the Rules of the Supreme Court, Ord. 11. The court, however, retains an overriding discretion to refuse to hear the dispute in both these situations where there is no sufficient connection between the subject matter of the dispute and this country or its law, or if the litigation would be more conveniently and appropriately brought before a foreign court. Furthermore, if proceedings in respect of the dispute have already been commenced in a foreign court, an English court will not usually permit concurrent proceedings to be initiated in England by the plaintiff or the defendant in the foreign proceedings, unless the dispute has a closer connection with England or its law than with the country where the foreign proceedings are pending, or unless there is a clear and legitimate advantage to the plaintiff in the English proceedings for them to be conducted here.

The 1968 Convention

The 1968 Convention on Jurisdiction and the Enforcement of Judgments enables the courts of a Convention country to entertain litigation if any one of several alternative conditions is satisfied. It is, therefore, possible under the Convention for the courts of two or more Convention countries to have jurisdiction over a dispute concurrently because different alternative conditions are satisfied in respect of each of them. Exclusive jurisdiction is given by the Convention to the courts of one Convention country alone only in respect of certain proceedings relating to status, land and industrial property rights[2], and these clearly do not include proceedings relating to bank accounts. It is possible under the Convention for conflicting judgments to be given in two or more Convention countries on the

---

2. 1968 Convention on Jurisdiction and the Enforcement of Judgments, Art. 16.

same dispute relating to a bank account. The resulting impasse is partially resolved by absolving a Convention country from its obligation to recognise and enforce a judgment properly given in another Convention country, if it is irreconcilable with a judgment given by one of the first country's courts[3].

The first and universal condition for a court to have jurisdiction over any dispute under the Convention is that the defendant or respondent is domiciled in the country of that court[4]. 'Domiciled' for this purpose has the meaning attributed to it by the national law of that country[5], and the Civil Jurisdiction and Judgments Act 1982, ss. 41 and 42 define 'domiciled' for the purpose of the Convention in a manner quite different from the normal meaning of the term. An individual is domiciled in that part of the United Kingdom where he is resident in a way which indicates that he has a substantial connection with that part. If he has been resident there for three months or more, it is presumed, unless the contrary is proved, that he is domiciled there[6]. A corporation (including a company) is domiciled in the Convention country where it has its seat[7], and its seat will be treated as situate in the United Kingdom if it was incorporated or has its registered office in any part of the United Kingdom, or if its central management and control (i.e. the habitual meeting place of its board of directors) is in any part of the United Kingdom[8]. The part of the United Kingdom where a corporation has its seat will be that part (England and Wales, Scotland or Northern Ireland) where it has its registered office (if it is a company) or an official address (if it is a statutory or chartered corporation), or where its central management or control is exercised or where it has a place of business[9]. It is, therefore, possible for a United Kingdom company to be domiciled for the purpose of the Convention concurrently in all three parts of the United Kingdom.

The remaining alternative conditions under the Convention for the exercise of jurisdiction by the courts of a Convention country depend on the nature of the cause of action alleged, and not on the status of either or any of the parties, beyond the fact that the defendant or respondent must be domiciled (in the sense explained above) in one of the Convention countries, but not necessarily the

3. Ibid. Art. 27.
4. Ibid. Art. 2.
5. Ibid. Arts. 52(1) and 53(1).
6. Civil Jurisdiction and Judgments Act 1982, s. 41(2), (3) and (6).
7. Convention, Art. 53(1).
8. CJJA 1982, s. 42(2) and (3).
9. Ibid. s. 42(4).

country in which the proceedings are brought[10]. Disputes relating to bank accounts may fall under any of three of the alternative conditions based on the cause of action, the remaining four alternative jurisdictional conditions being irrelevant. The three alternative conditions which may apply are[11]: (a) that the dispute relates to a contractual obligation which was to be performed in the Convention country where the proceedings are brought (e.g. the contractual obligation of a bank to repay the credit balance of an account at a specified place in that country, or at a branch of the bank in that country); (b) that the dispute relates to a tort which was committed in the Convention country where the proceedings are brought (e.g. an action brought against a bank for carrying out the mandate of an account holder in a negligent manner causing loss to him or to a third party to whom the bank owes a duty of care); or (c) that the dispute arises out of the operations of a branch, agency or other establishment of the defendant in the Convention country where the proceedings are brought (e.g. an action brought against a bank to recover loss caused by the inaccurate despatch, transmission or implementation of the account holder's instructions to make payments out of the account by a branch of the bank in the Convention country where the proceedings are instituted).

Where proceedings have been properly instituted in a Convention country against a defendant or respondent, it is possible for other persons to be made either: (a) co-defendants, or additional respondents, if the claims against them arise from the same transactions or acts or omissions as those alleged to give rise to a cause of action against the initial defendant or respondent; (b) third parties against whom any of the defendants claims an indemnity, a contribution, or damages arising out of the same transactions, or acts or omissions, as the claim against any of the original defendants; or (c) additional defendants to a counterclaim against the plaintiff brought by a defendant to the plaintiff's action, but only if the counterclaim arises from the same transactions, or acts or omissions, as the plaintiff's claim against that defendant[12]. If a person is to be added as a co-defendant, a third party or a defendant to a counterclaim in these circumstances, however, he must be domiciled in a Convention country in the sense explained above[13].

An example of this rule, extending the persons who may be added

---

10. Convention, Art. 5.
11. Ibid. Art. 5(1), (3) and (5).
12. Ibid. Art. 6.
13. Ibid. Art. 6.

as parties to proceedings brought under the Convention in relation to a bank account, is where an action is brought by the beneficiary of a letter of credit issued by a bank at the request of its customer, when a confirming bank in another Convention country has confirmed the letter of credit, but has refused to take up the shipping documents tendered by the beneficiary and to pay or accept bills of exchange for the amount of the credit. If the beneficiary sues the issuing bank in the appropriate Convention country, that bank may have the confirming bank joined as a co-defendant to the action (because the two banks are severally liable under the same obligations created by the letter of credit), or as a third party (if the confirming bank's rejection of the shipping documents was wrongful, and it is therefore liable to indemnify the issuing bank against its liability to the beneficiary). An example of the joinder of a third person as a defendant to a counterclaim relating to a bank account is where a customer of a bank in a Convention country sues it to recover the credit balance of his account, and the bank counterclaims for the debit balance on another overdrawn account, held by the same customer, which has been guaranteed by a third person who is added as an additional defendant to the counterclaim. In all these situations the person who is made an additional party to the proceedings must be domiciled in a Convention country, but not necessarily the Convention country where the original plaintiff or defendant is domiciled, or the Convention country with which the plaintiff's cause of action is connected.

Finally, it is possible for the parties to a dispute, any one or more of whom are domiciled in a Convention country, to agree that the courts of a particular Convention country, or a particular court of that country, shall have exclusive jurisdiction over disputes which have arisen or which may arise in connection with a particular legal relationship between them[14]. In order to be effective to give exclusive jurisdiction to the designated court or courts, however, the agreement between the parties to the relationship or the dispute arising out of it must be in writing, or must be evidenced in writing. If the relationship or dispute concerns international trade or commerce, the agreement must be in a form accepted in the branch of international trade or commerce in which the parties are engaged (e.g. telex messages or, in international banking transactions, SWIFT messages)[15]. It should be noted that the agreement must give *exclusive* jurisdiction

14. This need not necessarily be a contractual relationship: Convention, Art. 17, first para.
15. Ibid., Art. 17, first para.

to the courts, or a particular court of a Convention country, and if it conforms to the formal requirement of the Convention, it is effective to give jurisdiction to the designated court, or courts, to the exclusion of all other courts in Convention countries which would otherwise have jurisdiction. Thus are the standard general business conditions employed by all German banks made sacrosanct, that the contract entered into by the bank and its customer when an account is opened shall be governed by German law, irrespective of the locality of the branch where the customer's account is held, and that all disputes arising under the contract shall be decided exclusively by the *Landgericht* (district court) of Frankfurt, Munich or any other West German city where the bank has its head office.

Jurisdiction outside the 1968 Convention

The 1968 Convention on Jurisdiction and the Enforcement of Judgments obviously does not provide a complete code governing the jurisdiction of the English courts over all disputes with a foreign element. Situations to which the Convention does not apply are still governed by the jurisdictional policy rules which the courts have established by case law and by the limiting factor that a writ or other originating process can be served out of the jurisdiction (i.e. outside England and Wales) only with the leave of the court under RSC, Ord. 11. There are no statutory rules defining the actions or proceedings with a foreign element which the English courts have jurisdiction to entertain, and at common law the limit of the jurisdiction of the English courts was set, not by reference to the subject matter of the proceedings, but by whether the person whom it was sought to sue or add as a party to the proceedings was present in England and Wales and so could be served. It was simply by a self-denying ordinance that the courts determined, as a matter of policy, that even if service in England and Wales had been effected, they would not hear the action if there was no sufficient connection between its subject matter and this country (geographical connection) and English law was not applicable (legal connection), or if the courts of another country were the more appropriate and convenient forum for the proceedings (*forum non conveniens*).

Order 11, rule 1 is concerned not directly with the jurisdiction of the High Court of Justice in disputes with a foreign element, but with the power of the court in its discretion to permit the service of a writ or other originating process on a party outside England and

Wales. The circumstances in which leave can be given are listed exhaustively in Ord. 11, and so it is not possible for the court to give leave in a situation which is not within the order. Nevertheless, even if the cause of action is within the order, the court will only give leave to serve the writ or originating process outside the jurisdiction in the same circumstances as it would entertain an action commenced by a writ which had been served within England and Wales. Consequently, the three factors mentioned in the preceding paragraph are material when the court considers whether to give leave to serve a writ or originating process outside England and Wales. The only difference between an application for leave to serve process outside the jurisdiction, and an application to the court by a defendant who has been served with a writ or other process within the jurisdiction to stay the proceedings, is that the burden of satisfying the court that leave to serve outside the jurisdiction should be given rests on the plaintiff or applicant, whereas on an application to stay proceedings where service in England and Wales has already been effected, the burden of satisfying the court that the action should not be allowed to proceed rests on the defendant.

A defendant need not obtain leave of the court to serve a counter-claim on the plaintiff out of the jurisdiction, because by bringing the action the plaintiff impliedly agrees to submit to the jurisdiction of the court to entertain counterclaims[16]. However, a defendant must obtain leave if he is to serve a third party notice outside the jurisdiction on a person who is not already a party to the proceedings, or to add such a person as an additional defendant to a counterclaim[17].

Of the 16 situations listed in Ord. 11, r. 1(1) where the court may give leave to serve a writ or other process out of the jurisdiction, only five are relevant in relation to proceedings concerning bank accounts. The first is where the proceedings are for an injunction ordering the defendant to do, or abstain from doing, any act within England and Wales (e.g. an injunction to prevent a foreign bank from transferring a customer's funds held with a London agent bank to the foreign bank abroad). The second situation is where the proceedings relate to a contract which was made in England and Wales, or through an agent of the defendant residing or trading there, who acted on behalf of a non-resident principal, or where the contract is governed by English law or contains a provision by which

16. *Derby & Co. Ltd* v *Larsson* [1976] 1 WLR 202.
17. *Swansea Shipping Co.* v *Duncan* (1876) 1 QBD 644; *Speller* v *Bristol Steam Navigation Co.* (1884) 13 QBD 96; *Wilson & Co.* v *Balcarres Brook Steamship Co.* [1893] 1 QB 422.

the High Court shall have jurisdiction (not necessarily exclusive jurisdiction) over actions brought under it (e.g. an action by a customer of a foreign bank to recover the credit balance of an account held by him with a branch of the bank in England). The third situation is where the action is brought for a breach of contract committed within England and Wales, whether the contract was made within or outside the jurisdiction, and whether the contract has also been broken abroad or not (e.g. failure to repay a deposit made with a foreign bank which promised to repay it with interest either abroad or in London at the depositor's option, when the depositor has requested and been refused payment in London). The fourth situation is where the action is in respect of a tort committed within England and Wales or resulting in damages being sustained there by the plaintiff (e.g. the negligent collection in England and Wales by a foreign bank of a bill of exchange or cheque drawn on, or accepted by, a London bank in favour of the plaintiff, when the foreign bank's customer has no title to the bill or cheque). The fifth and final situation is where the action is brought to enforce a security over land or movable property (whether tangible or intangible) in England and Wales (e.g. an action brought by a bank to recover the amount overdrawn on the account of a foreign customer out of the proceeds of a charge created by him over trade debts owed to him by his customers resident in England).

It will be noted that the circumstances where the court can give leave to serve a writ or other originating process outside England and Wales are somewhat wider than those in which an action, or proceedings falling under the 1968 Convention on Jurisdiction and the Enforcement of Judgments, can be brought before an English court. This is particularly so in respect of contracts, which under Ord. 11, r. 1(1) need not be performable in England and Wales if they were made there, or were made by or through, an agent of the defendant who was resident or trading there, or if they are governed by English law, or where any breach of the contract is alleged to have occurred in England and Wales. The greater width of Ord. 11, r. 1(1), however, is limited by the discretion of the court to refuse leave to serve a writ or originating process outside the jurisdiction, and in practice it is found that the 1968 Convention is rather more liberal in enabling plaintiffs to commence proceedings in an English court as of right, than the High Court is in exercising its power to permit the service of writs outside the jurisdiction. It should, of course, be observed that if an action falls within the 1968 Convention but cannot, under its provisions, be brought in an English court, it is not possible for an application to be made to the court under

Ord. 11, r. 1(1) for leave to serve a writ or other originating process outside the jurisdiction. The Convention is exhaustive in regulating the jurisdiction of the courts of the Convention countries in respect of proceedings falling within it, and since the Convention is part of United Kingdom law by statute[18], it is not possible for the High Court to exercise jurisdiction in a case falling within the Convention but not allocated by it to the courts of England and Wales, by permitting the plaintiff to serve the writ or process initiating the action outside the jurisdiction under Ord. 11.

THE SYSTEM OF LAW WHICH GOVERNS A BANK ACCOUNT

The proper determination of the system of law which governs the legal relationship between a bank and a person who has an account with it may be material in deciding any one of three questions, namely: (a) whether the courts of a country have jurisdiction to decide disputes about the rights and obligations of the bank and the customer as regards each other; (b) what rules of law must be applied to resolve such disputes; and (c) where the credit or debit balance of the account must be treated as situate to be subject to the claims of third persons (including the state) or to impose collateral obligations on third persons (e.g. the claims of the account holder's creditors or of his secured creditors who claim a charge over the credit balance of the account; the liability of the heirs or other universal successors of an account holder under a civil law system for the amount overdrawn by the holder on his bank account). The English courts have worked out their solution to this problem through a succession of judicial decisions which have been purely pragmatic and have evolved two alternative solutions which the courts have applied according to the facts of each case. Where United Kingdom statute law has intervened (e.g. in respect of the disposal of enemy-owned property in wartime), the statutory rules override the judge-made criteria, of course, but in the absence of applicable United Kingdom statutory prescription, the judge-made criteria apply, and this is particularly important in deciding whether English law will recognise foreign legislation or government executive acts as effective in relation to bank accounts.

A number of English decisions have held that a credit or debit

18. Civil Jurisdiction and Judgments Act 1982, s. 2(1).

balance on a bank account is legally situate in the country where the balance is recoverable, and the rights and obligations of the bank and the account holder are governed by the law of that country[19]. This test has the merit of consistency with the general rule that a debt is situate in, and is governed by the law of, the country where proceedings would normally be brought against the debtor to recover it, and this is so even if the debtor has an option to discharge the debt by paying it elsewhere[20]. Credit and debit balances on bank accounts are treated in all countries as debts payable on demand, or on the giving of an agreed length of notice, or on the arrival of an agreed date for payment, and the treatment of bank account balances as debts for conflict of law purposes helps towards achieving uniformity in the conflict of laws treatment of balances on bank accounts throughout the world.

In a number of other decisions the English courts have held that a credit or debit balance of a bank account is governed by the law of the country where the debtor (bank or customer) resides, and it is deemed to be legally situate in that country[21]. The normal meaning of 'residence' in the case of a bank (which will always take the form of a company or partnership) is the place where the central control and management of the bank's affairs is situate, and it is treated in conflict of laws situations as being resident in the country where that place is situate[22]. But in the context of accounts held with a bank, the courts have equated the bank's residence with its head or principal office, although in all the relevant cases that was also the place where its directors met to manage its affairs[23]. However, this latter test of residence causes uncertainty if the bank has several branches in different countries, and in cases where the relevant account was held at a branch of the bank in a country different from that where its head office was situate, the courts which have adopted the criterion

---

19. *Adelaide Electric Supply Co. Ltd* v *Prudential Assurance Co. Ltd* [1934] AC 122; *Re Russo Asiatic Bank* [1934] Ch 720; *Auckland Corpn* v *Alliance Assurance Co. Ltd* [1937] AC 587; *F & K Jabbour* v *Custodian of Israeli Absentee Property* [1954] 1 WLR 139; *Re Banque des Marchands de Moscou (No. 2)* [1954] 1 WLR 1108; *Power Curber International Ltd* v *Nationa. Bank of Kuwait SAK* [1981] 1 WLR 1233; *Brooks Associates Incorpd* v *Basu* [1983] QB 220.
20. *Rossano* v *Manufacturers Life Assurance Co.* [1963] 2 QB 352.
21. *New York Life Insurance Co.* v *Public Trustee* [1924] 2 Ch 101; *Re Claim by Helbert Wagg Ltd* [1956] Ch 323.
22. *Swedish Central Railway Co. Ltd* v *Thompson* [1925] AC 495; *Unit Construction Co. Ltd* v *Bullock* [1960] AC 351; *Dreyfus* v *IRC* (1929) 14 TC 560.
23. *Re Maudslay Sons and Field Ltd* [1900] 1 Ch 602; *Martin* v *Nadel* [1906] 2 KB 26; *Clare & Co.* v *Dresdner Bank* [1915] 2 KB 576; *Joachimson* v *Swiss Bank Corpn* [1921] 3 KB 110.

of residence have treated the bank as resident in the country where its branch is situated at which the account was kept[24]. Fortunately, the location of the branch of a bank where an account is kept usually coincides with the place where any credit balance of the account is payable to the account holder, and also with the place where any debit balance is payable by him to the bank. Consequently, whichever of the two criteria is applied to determine the system of law which governs a bank account and its legal location, the place of recoverability or the location of the branch where the account is kept, the answer is the same. In a recent decision, *Libyan Arab Foreign Bank* v *Bankers Trust Company*[25], Staughton J abandoned the residence test for the location of a bank account with all its ambiguities, and opted instead for the simpler, more direct and more certain test of the situation of the branch of the bank where the account in question was kept at the relevant time. He held that the relationship and obligations of the bank and the account holder are governed, in the absence of a contrary agreement, by the law of the country where that branch is situate, and the account is to be treated as located in the same country. It is to be hoped that this simplified test is adopted uniformly by the courts in the future.

24. *R* v *Lovitt* [1912] AC 212; *Richardson* v *Richardson* [1927] P 228; *Arab Bank Ltd* v *Barclays Bank (DCO) Ltd* [1954] AC 495.
25. [1987] 2 FTLR 509; [1988] 1 Lloyd's Rep. 259.

SET-OFF AND THE CONFLICT OF LAWS[1]

Philip R Wood

CLASSIFICATIONS OF SET-OFF

Set-off is the discharge of a creditor's claim ('the creditor's (primary) claim') against a debtor by a claim owed by the creditor to the debtor ('the cross-claim'). The debtor uses his asset to discharge his liability. Thus a bank sets off a loan owed to it by a customer against a deposit which the bank owes to the customer. The bank does not apply the deposit to pay the loan because the bank has no property in the deposit.

The types of set-off may be conveniently labelled by the use of non-legal terms as follows:

(a) Independent set-off

This is the set-off of liquidated, unconnected or independent claims originally authorised in England by the Statutes of Set-off of 1729 and 1735. In civilian and Roman states, this prime form of set-off is generally called compensation. In England this set-off is primarily exercisable in judicial proceedings, subject to exceptions in favour of those entitled to general liens in similar circumstances, such as banks and brokers, and is non-retroactive to the time the claims were first eligible for set-off for the purposes of default in payment, interest and limitation. In Napoleonic regimes the set-off is automatic, as in France, Luxembourg, Belgium, Mexico and Panama. In the Germanic regimes, such as West Germany, Japan, Korea and the Scandinavian countries, the set-off may be declared extrajudicially by the debtor and is retroactive.

(b) Transaction set-off

This is the set-off of transactionally related claims and is referred to in England as equitable set-off or abatement, and in the United States as recoupment. Examples are the right of a charterer to reduce

1. This article is based on Chapter 23 of *English and International Set-off* 1989, Sweet & Maxwell, by Philip R. Wood.

hire by virtue of a cross-claim for wrongful withholding of or defects in the vessel and the right of a buyer to set-off damages for defects in the goods. Everywhere this set-off is self-help and either, or both, claims may be unliquidated.

(c)   Current account set-off
This is the set-off of current accounts, mainly between a bank and a customer (sometimes called combination in England). The set-off is universally self-help.

(d)   Contractual set-off
This is a right of set-off created by contract in circumstances in which such right would not otherwise exist, e.g. set-off of independent unliquidated claims or immature claims or a self-help independent set-off.

(e)   Insolvency set-off
This is a right of set-off arising where one debtor–creditor is insolvent. The common law and Germanic jurisdictions confer a very wide set-off on insolvency but in a large bloc of Napoleonic states, insolvency set-off is not permitted except in the case of 'connexity' (transaction set-off) or current account set-off. These states include France, Luxembourg, Belgium, Spain, Greece and most Latin American states, except Panama. Austria and Italy allow insolvency set-off. In England insolvency set-off is governed by s. 323 of the Insolvency Act 1986 (for individuals) and Rule 4.90 of the Insolvency Rules 1986 (for companies) – the 'insolvency set-off clause'.

SOLVENT SET-OFF

Generally

There is virtually no jurisprudence in England in relation to the conflict of laws position on solvent set-off, and what little case law there is precedes the flowering of English private international law. As a result one can only make a number of suggestions[2].

---

2. See especially Lando, *International Encyclopaedia of Comparative Law*, 1977, vol. III, chapter 24, para. 222, et seq.; Rabel-Bernstein, *Conflict of Laws*, vol. III 475.

Independent set-off

Generally It is suggested that, as a broad general principle, the question of whether a claim has been discharged by independent set-off should be governed by the law of the claim which the debtor asserts has been discharged, subject to any public policy rules of the forum to the contrary and to any particular circumstances requiring a different solution. In practice, this will ordinarily lead to the result that, in any judicial proceedings to test the availability of the set-off, the court should apply the law of the plaintiff's claim—the creditor's primary claim—to determine whether the debtor was entitled to discharge the creditor's claim by set-off. It will also follow that the effect of the set-off (for example, whether a declaration is retroactive) will be determined by that law. The courts should not apply the *lex fori* except in relation to purely procedural matters. Notwithstanding this, the English law of independent set-off may not have reached the point of treating it as predominantly substantive in its effect and may conservatively give priority to its procedural aspect. If so, the English courts may apply the *lex fori*.

Principle conflicting issues The principle issues likely to involve conflicting rules of law in relation to independent set-off include:

(a) Whether the set-off is self-help, i.e. whether tender of the creditor's primary claim by the debtor after the deduction of the debtor's cross-claim is valid legal tender. On the one hand, common law systems on the whole do not permit solvent self-help independent set-off (except by debtor-creditors entitled to general liens), but freely allow current account and transaction set-off as self-help remedies. On the other hand, many civil code jurisdictions allow self-help independent set-off as a form of extrajudicial payment, with or without a declaration.

(b) The conditions of the availability of the set-off, in particular the degree of liquidity; whether multi-currency set-off is available; whether a set-off of an immature cross-claim is permitted if the creditor's financial position is precarious; and whether the cross-claim must have matured before the creditor's primary claim or before the creditor commences suit for his primary claim.

(c) Whether the creditor's primary claim is insulated, protected or exempt from set-off, e.g. freight, wages, alimony or a claim for a tort, and whether the debtor's cross-claim is ineligible for set-off, e.g. because of a statute of limitations.

(d) The manner in which the set-off is exercised if self-help, e.g. automatic or by declaration.

(e) The effect of the set-off, in particular whether it operates retroactively to the time the conditions of set-off existed so as to cause interest to stop running, to prevent the debtor from being in default (damages, repudiation, forfeitures, accelerations, withdrawals, foreclosures) and also, if the reciprocal claims are payable at different places, whether the debtor must compensate the creditor for the costs of transmission (as is the case in many civilian jurisdictions).

(f) The appropriation or imputation of set-offs to a plurality of obligations owed by the debtor to the creditor.

It should be emphasised that no single rule should necessarily apply to all of these situations and particular circumstances may dictate different solutions.

In principle the main systems of law available for determining these questions are the law of the creditor's primary claim, the law of the debtor's cross-claim, the cumulative law of the primary claim and the cross-claim, and the *lex fori*. One can disregard the law of the place of performance, the law of the contracting parties and the law of the place of contract as not being serious contenders for one reason or another. It may be said that the law of the place where the creditor's primary claim is payable should be influential but this in principle is considered doubtful and does not seem to enjoy any approval among the writers.

Role of lex fori The *lex fori* is not considered the appropriate system of law to determine the availability or effects of independent set-off for several reasons. The arguments would be that, first, a set-off is predominantly a matter of substance. It is a form of payment or discharge or extinction of an obligation and this is a substantive matter in conflict of laws which is governed by proper law doctrines, not the *lex fori*. Set-off is not primarily a procedural convenience to avoid circuity of action, although the objectives of judicial economy are present. The substantive nature of independent set-off is revealed by the fact that, for example, the original Statutes of Set-off of 1729 and 1735 were passed partly to prevent the imprisonment of debtors who, on a taking of the overall accounts between the parties, really owed nothing. Going to jail is plainly a matter of substance and not just of judicial economy. The present day analogy is the question of whether the debtor is in default for non-payment—which is a substantive matter.

The mere fact that the remedy is usually, in England, available only in judicial proceedings should not convert a substantive right into a mere matter of procedure. Independent set-off is so nearly extrajudicial in England that a creditor is penalised by costs if he does not deduct his claim in bringing his action. Transaction set-off is clearly a substantive right protecting the debtor against a creditor claiming for something which he has not done or has done defectively[3]. Abatement has always been regarded as a substantive defence. Lord Diplock said[4] that abatement was 'no mere procedural rule designed to avoid circuity of action but a substantive defence at common law ...' But the policies of transaction set-off are different from independent set-off.

Secondly, the application of the *lex fori* would make little sense where both reciprocal claims are governed by a foreign system of law, whether different or the same. Thirdly, as a general principle of modern conflict of laws, the *lex fori* should not be applied, unless there is no convenient alternative, because it elevates the rules of the home forum above all others and might encourage forum-shopping. The homeward trend is to be discouraged as inimical to the expectations of the parties and to the recognition of legitimate foreign interests. Generally the role played by the *lex fori* in conflict of laws doctrine is on the retreat in England[5].

However, the *lex fori* should govern some matters which may be regarded as primarily procedural. These should include whether a set-off which is erroneously pleaded as a counterclaim can still qualify for the advantages of set-off and the time by which the set-off must be pleaded as a defence. An argument can be made either way as to whether the English rule that a cross-claim not due and payable when the plaintiff commences his action for the primary claim does not qualify for independent set-off should be regarded as procedural or substantive. One view is that this technicality ought to be procedural because it relates to the convenient disposition of judicial business and the time of pleading. The contrary argument is that the

---

3. See *Hanak v Green* [1958] 2 All ER 141, CA; *The Leon* [1985] 2 Lloyd's Rep 470.
4. In *Gilbert Ash (Northern) Ltd v Modern Engineering (Bristol) Ltd* [1971] 3 All ER 195, HL, at 216.
5. See *Dicey & Morris The Conflict of Laws*, 11th ed., p. 173 (hereafter called Dicey).

rule reflects the idea that a cross-claim must be mature before it can be set off, which is a matter of substance.

Law of primary claim and cumulative law compared The argument in favour of the law of the claim asserted to be paid is principally that the manner in which the debtor pays the creditor's primary claim—the question of discharge—should be governed by the law of that claim in conformity with the general principle that the proper law governs the discharge of a contract: Dicey, rule 187. It is understood that German law adopts this solution[6].

The difficulty is that set-off pays both debts, both the creditor's primary claim and the debtor's cross-claim, and therefore it may be said that the law governing the cross-claim should also be considered. This has led some writers to support the cumulation of laws, i.e. that the availability of set-off depends upon it being available under the law governing both the primary claim and the law governing the cross-claim. It is said that one argument in favour of this is that set-off is an unusual method of debt extinction and should be administered with caution. Another is that the cumulation of laws will afford greater predictability because, until a set-off is declared, one cannot tell which of the reciprocal claims is the primary claim and therefore which law will apply[7]. But this is perhaps not usually so in practice because generally only one party asserts the set-off unless the set-off is agreed or unless *both* claims allow automatic extinction in which case no conflict arises. Further, if one examines specific situations it would seem that the application of the law of the primary claim does confer a measure of predictability in the actual result.

Where one law allows a set-off but the other does not, this may often result in one of the parties always being the loser. The holder of the claim which is most favourable to set-off will normally have an advantage, whoever brings suit.

Example
A owes B a loan. B owes A a damages claim for breach of a foreign exchange contract where the damages are readily ascertainable. The law of the loan permits A to set off a cross-claim for readily ascertainable unliquidated damages but the law of the damages claim does not permit illiquid set-off.

6. BGH, decision of 22 November 1962; 38 BGH 2 254, 256; Higher Court of Appeal Frankfurt, decision of 27 October 1966, 1967 NJW 501; Provincial Court of Hamburg, decision of 16 November 1973, 1974 AWD 410; BBr 56.
7. Lando, op. cit. appears to favour cumulative laws.

If B claims the loan from A and if one applies the law of the loan as the primary claim, A will have a set-off.

If conversely A claims the damages from B, the law of this primary claim precludes B from setting off the loan.

The result is that in the first case B is met by a set-off and so is not paid and in the second case he is deprived of a set-off.

If one reverses the laws, so that the law of the loan disallows set-off but the law of the damages claim allows the remedy, it will be seen that now A is always the loser because if he sues B, he is met by a set-off, but if B sues him, he cannot set off.

If the cumulative law were applied, in neither case would there be a set-off.

One old English case suggests the application of the law of the creditor's primary claim to determine the availability of set-off. The case concerned the question of whether a guarantor can use a set-off which the principal debtor has against the principal creditor. In many civilian jurisdictions the code specifically allows this in the case of independent set-off.

In *Allen* v *Kemble*[8] JC, a resident in Demerara drew a bill of exchange in favour of B, also resident in Demerara, payable in London, upon C, resident in Scotland, and C accepted the same, making it payable in London. B indorsed the bill to D who shortly afterwards became bankrupt. When C's acceptance became due, he held two bills of exchange accepted by D, which were dishonoured and protested for non-payment. D's assignees did not proceed against C but brought an action in Demerara against A and B, the drawer and indorser, who pleaded a right of set-off to the extent of the two bills accepted by D.

Held: First, the bill having been drawn in Demerara, the Roman-Dutch law in force in that colony must govern the case. By that law the bill accepted by C was compensated or extinguished *pro tanto* by the bills accepted by D. Secondly, a surety was entitled to avail himself of this rule of law in respect of a debt due to the principal debtor; and, thirdly, the drawer and indorser were to be deemed sureties for the acceptor and entitled to plead this right of set-off.

The above case is inconclusive because the *lex fori* where the action was originally brought and the governing law of the 'guarantee', i.e.

8. (1848) 6 Moo BC 314.

the creditor's primary claim, were the same, namely, Demerara. Further, *Meyer v Dresser*[9], cited below, contains *obiter dicta* that the *lex fori* governs. The case was on a wholly different point and is not considered dispositive.

Where the issue is whether the set-off is retroactive to the date both claims were eligible for set-off (which primarily determines whether the creditor can forfeit property, cancel a policy, withdraw a chartered ship or leased equipment, accelerate a credit or enforce a mortgage for non-payment of the creditor's primary claim), it is considered that the law governing that claim should be applicable— the law of the loan, the law of the insurance policy, the law of the charterparty—subject to any public policy rules of the forum to the contrary. That law should also apply in determining whether or not the set-off is retroactive as regards interest on that claim and the general default implications. Again, in practice this will generally result in the law of the creditor's primary claim being applicable.

Example
A bank owes a deposit to a customer. The law governing the deposit allows an extrajudicial declaratory set-off which is retro-active to the date the reciprocal claims matured in a form eligible for independent set-off. The customer owes a loan to the bank. Under the law governing the loan, the set-off may be pleaded only in judicial proceedings and the set-off is not retroactive.
The deposit falls due and the customer declares a set-off against an instalment of the loan. The bank accelerates the loan for non-payment because under the law of the loan the payment by set-off is not valid legal tender.
If the bank sues for the accelerated amount, the law of the loan should govern because that is the claim which the debtor asserts has been paid and the manner of payment should be controlled by the law of the loan, not the deposit. The bank should succeed.
If, conversely, the bank by declaration sets off the loan instalment against the deposit and the customer sues for the deposit, the customer will not succeed because under the law of the deposit an extrajudicial declaratory set-off is permitted.

Insulated claims   In the case of insulated claims, such as freight or (in some jurisdictions) wages, pensions, alimony and other support claims, the policies are likely to vary according to the claim concerned but generally the application of the law of the creditor's primary

9. (1864) 16 CB (NS) 646.

claim should produce the right result in many cases, subject to public policy rules.

Where the claim is insulated with a view to protecting the creditor, as in the case of claims for wages or alimony, the application of the law of the creditor's primary claim achieves a satisfactory result except where the policy of the law is to prevent the creditor from voluntarily foregoing the protection of the law if he wishes to.

Example
An employer owes wages to an employee which under the law of the employment contract are insulated from set-off. The employee works in a foreign branch and owes the employer a cross-claim for a railway season ticket loan and under the law of that cross-claim, the wages would not be insulated from set-off. If the employee sues for his wages, the law of the insulated claim—the creditor's primary claim—should apply so as to prevent set-off. If the employer sues for the ticket loan, the law of the primary claim—the ticket loan—will enable him to set off unpaid wages. The result of this is that the employee can choose to forego his wages, but the employer cannot compel him to do so. But this result should not be permitted if it offended the policy of the forum in ensuring that wages always reach the employee in cash whether he likes it or not.

There is one inconclusive English case on an insulated claim for freight: strictly this was a case of transaction set-off.

In *Meyer* v *Dresser*[10], a merchant sought to deduct a damages claim for short delivery from his liability for freight.
Held: The contract of carriage was governed by English law and freight is insulated from solvent set-off under English law. Hence the merchant could not deduct. But the court made a number of suggestions—all of which were *obiter*—that set-off is a matter of procedure and therefore governed by the *lex fori*. But apparently the point was admitted and, as mentioned above, the role of the *lex fori* is now dwindling.

Willes J said, at 665:
'The set-off being admitted to be a matter of procedure, we cannot introduce a case of set-off from the Prussian law simply because the contract sued on is a Prussian contract.'

10. (1864) 16 CB (NS) 646.

Byles J said, at 665:

'[It] seems to me, as had already been remarked by my Lord and my learned brother Willes, *that this is a matter of procedure*. It has been decided over and over again in this country that the Statute of Limitations is matter of procedure, and is to be governed by the law of the country where the remedy is sought, and that the *lex loci* prevails. It has been held in America that the law of set-off is a portion of the procedure; and, my Lord informs me, in this country also.'

Where, as in the above case, the insulated claim is for freight, it is considered that again the right result is reached if the law governing the creditor's primary claim is applied. If the carrier sues for insulated freight, the merchant cannot set off. Where the merchant sues for another claim, the carrier can set off freight.

If the insulated claim is a negotiable instrument and is insulated from set-off by its governing law, then, if the creditor—being the first holder of the instrument and not a transferee—sues on the instrument, there should be no set-off. If the debtor sues the creditor for another claim, the creditor should be permitted to set off the instrument.

If the insulated claim is a letter of credit or bank 'first demand' guarantee and if the beneficiary claims, the question of whether the issuing bank can set off should be governed by the law of the letter of credit or guarantee as the law of the primary claim. If, conversely, the bank claims another debt from the beneficiary, the question of whether the beneficiary can set off the liability of the bank on the letter of credit or guarantee should be governed by the law of the bank's claim, not by the law of the letter of credit or the guarantee or the cumulative law.

Where the claim is insulated by a contract prohibiting set-off, the proper law of that contract should apply in accordance with the general rules of conflict of laws applicable to contracts. The forum should not impose its own views of judicial economy to override the bargain of the parties other than in an exceptional case. The forum should impose only its public policy rules, e.g. imperative statutes protecting consumers.

Where the claim is insulated by statute or rule of law because it is a governmental claim for taxes, the application of the law of the governmental claim will generally uphold the policy in a case where the government claims the unpaid tax. In the ordinary case this situation will arise domestically where local statute will govern in any event because courts will not generally entertain claims by foreign revenue authorities for taxes.

Ineligible debtor cross-claims

The conflicts rules for the various ineligible debtor cross-claims, such as time-barred or claims valid but unenforceable by action because of a formal defect, will naturally differ according to the cross-claim concerned.

Where the issue is whether a debtor has discharged the creditor's primary claim by a self-help set-off for the purposes of a limitation statute, the law of the primary claim should govern. If, on the one hand, under the law of the creditor's primary claim, which he subsequently sues for, the set-off operated as payment within the limitation period for the cross-claim, the creditor should have no claim. If, on the other hand, under the law of the creditor's claim the set-off is not payment—as in the case of English law—again the application of the law of the creditor's primary claim will yield the right result[11].

Where a plaintiff is entitled to immunity, it is expected that the English courts will apply the State Immunity Act 1978. A sovereign submitting to the jurisdiction of the English courts by suing in England submits to related counterclaims and should also be deemed to submit to independent set-offs. It is considered that all questions of set-off in relation to immunity from suit and enforcement should be *lex fori*. Particular facts may determine a different solution.

Current account and transaction set-off

Generally, the conflicts rules in relation to current account set-off should be similar to those relating to independent set-off. In practice the accounts will generally be maintained at the same office and be subject to the same system of law.

Similarly, conflicts issues are not likely to arise in relation to transaction set-off because both the primary claim and the cross-claim will usually be governed by the same law of the transaction. But, if this were not the case, the independent set-off principles should be considered. It has already been observed that the courts

11. Consider also the Foreign Limitation Periods Act 1984.

have stated that both forms of transaction set-off, abatement and equitable set-off, are substantive.

Contractual set-off

The efficacy of a contract to set off should be governed by the law of the contract creating the set-off. The public policy, consumer protection, insolvency, stamp duty, exchange control, registration and other imperative rules of the forum may affect the efficacy of the contractual set-off.

It is suggested that the question of whether a creditor can charge back to his debtor the debt which the debtor owes the creditor should depend upon the law of the debt which is charged back. Charge-backs appear to be universally available except in Australia, but their validity has recently been questioned in England, although without citation of relevant case law upholding charge-backs. Contractual set-off is the use of the debtor's asset to pay the debtor's liability: the bank sets off a loan against a deposit. A charge-back is the use of the creditor's asset to pay the creditor's liability: the bank has a security interest in the benefit of the deposit (the creditor's asset) and on enforcement merges this with the creditor–customer's liability on the loan (the creditor's liability and the bank's asset). In the case of assignments generally, it is thought that the law of the assigned debt governs assignability and the effects of the assignment, e.g. whether it is by way of security or absolute: see Dicey, rules 121 and 122 and the authorities there cited. Registrability will depend upon the territorial reach of the registration statute.

Counterclaims

The question of whether a cross-claim which does not qualify for a set-off may nevertheless be raised as a counterclaim should be entirely a matter for the *lex fori* since it concerns the convenience of the administration of judicial business. At least this appears to be the position in English law[12].

---

12. See *South African Republic* v *Compagnie Franco-Belge du Chemin de Fer du Nord* [1897] 2 Ch 487, CA.

INTERVENERS

Generally

One of the most important cases likely to arise in practice is whether set-off is protected against interveners—the main interveners being the assignee, the chargee, the attaching creditor, the pre-judgment attaching creditor, the undisclosed principal and the undisclosed beneficiary. The question here will be whether the debtor may set off, as against an intervener, a cross-claim owed to the debtor by his original creditor—the assignor, the chargor, the judgment debtor, the agent or the trustee. An example is where a bank owes a deposit to a customer and the customer assigns the deposit to a third party or the deposit is attached at a time when the customer owes a loan to the bank. It may well be that many jurisdictions will permit a set-off of a pre-notice cross-claim, qualifying for transaction, contractual and current account set-off but there appear to be significant differences of approach as regards independent set-off. The English position is refined.

As a very general proposition, not applicable to all cases, it is suggested that the question of whether a debtor may set off, as against an intervener, a cross-claim which the debtor has against the original or apparent creditor, should be governed by the law of the debt claimed by the intervener—the assignee, the undisclosed principal, or the undisclosed beneficiary. However, special considerations apply to attaching creditors and wronged beneficiaries.

Assignments

In relation to assignments, a preliminary point should be mentioned. Under the laws of some civil code jurisdictions an assignment is void as against creditors of the assignor (such as attaching creditors or creditors on insolvency) unless the assignment is notified to the debtor in the specified manner which is often formal. In England, notice is desirable for various purposes but notice is not necessary to assure the transfer of beneficial ownership as against attaching creditors of the assignor or as against the insolvency representative of the assignor.

Thus, under Art. 1690, French Civil Code, a formal signification by a *huissier* of the assignment to the debtor or an acceptance or acknowledgement of the transfer by the debtor by an *acte authentique* is required. A similar rule applies in Japan[13]. In the absence of these formalities, the assignment is wholly invalid, e.g. against creditors of the assignor, though it is effective as between assignor and assignee.

It is understood that, in the case of the French rule requiring formal notification for validity, German and Swiss decisions have determined the applicability of this requirement in accordance with the law of the debt assigned. If these decisions were followed in England, which they should be, and if the debt assigned were governed by a non-French law, the formality would not be necessary. However, if the debtor is located in France, the French courts apply the law of the debtor (since they maintain that the rule is for his protection) and insist on the formal notification so that, if it is not duly effected, local creditors are able to attach the debt in France and ignore the assignment. It is understood that the Japanese conflicts position, if the debtor is located in Japan, is the same.

In the absence of authority it is considered that where a debtor has a cross-claim against the assignor qualifying for set-off, the question of whether the assignee is subject to this set-off should be determined by the law of the assigned debt. The assignee should be able to look to that law in order to ascertain what set-offs he may be subject to. He cannot examine the laws of all potential cross-claims. The debtor should be able to look to the law of the obligation he owes to ascertain his vulnerability or otherwise to loss of set-off. This rule would also be consistent with the rule proposed in relation to independent set-off.

Undisclosed principals

In the case of undisclosed principals, it is considered that the law governing the obligation between the agent and the third party, which the undisclosed principal seeks to take over on intervention, should determine whether a cross-claim, which the third party has against the agent personally, is available for set-off against the principal. It would obviously be inappropriate to apply the law of the contract between the principal and the agent. If an undisclosed principal allows his agent to deal with third parties without disclosing his capacity, he should take the risk of the system of law under which the agent contracts with third parties[14].

---

13. See Art. 467, Japanese Civil Code; also, Korea CC Art. 450.
14. Consider *Maspons* v *Mildred* (1882) 9 QBD 530, CA; affd. sub. nom. *Mildred* v *Maspons* (1883) 8 App Cas 874 (a case on disclosed agency).

Garnishments

In the case of garnishments, while the English courts generally apply the *lex situs* to determine whether the debt is capable of being garnisheed, and to determine questions of the validity and effect of attachments or garnishments by foreign courts, it is suggested that the question of whether the garnishee can set off, as against the garnishor, a cross-claim which the garnishee has against the judgment debtor should be governed either by the *lex fori* or by the law of the attached claim. It would be more attractive, in the interests of the garnishee, to apply the law of the attached claim but often judicial enforcement is seen as the province of the *lex fori*. It is not considered that the *lex situs* of the attached debt should control, because the *lex situs* is relevant rather to the question of jurisdiction to attach: see Dicey, rule 124.

Where the parties have agreed a contractual set-off, the question of what law should govern the efficacy of that contract as against an attaching creditor appears to be undecided in England. If a foreign court claims jurisdiction to attach a debt and the contractual set-off is ineffective in that jurisdiction against the attaching creditor, it would not be surprising if in practice the foreign court applied its own mandatory rule avoiding the contract.

Undisclosed beneficiary

In the case of undisclosed beneficiaries, in those situations where the trustee is authorised not to disclose the trusteeship, similar principles should apply as in the case of undisclosed principals. Where the trustee is acting wrongfully, however, the position is likely to be different, see below.

MONEY AND PROPERTY CLAIMS

As a general proposition a debtor may not set off a pecuniary cross-claim against a demand which is proprietary in nature: there must be a debtor–creditor relationship both ways. Whether a claim is a money, or a proprietary claim in the case of conflict, will involve the conflicts rules relating to the particular issue. The subject is too large to debate here but the starting point would be to consult Dicey in relation to:

(a) transfers of beneficial ownership of property (such as sales)[15];
(b) trusts (such as claims for a beneficial interest or proceeds)[16];
(c) constructive trusts and restitutionary claims[17];
(d) torts giving rise to proprietary claims (such as wrongful interference with goods)[18].

INSOLVENCY SET-OFF

English insolvency proceedings

Under the Insolvency Act 1986 the English courts have jurisdiction to adjudge bankrupt any debtor in the cases laid down in s. 265, e.g. where the debtor is domiciled in England, is personally present in England on the day when the bankruptcy petition is presented, and in certain cases where he is resident here or carries on business here. Insolvent foreign companies may be wound up in various circumstances[19], e.g. if the foreign company has assets in England. There are special rules for companies in Scotland and Northern Ireland[20].

Insolvency set-off clause applies to all creditors claiming to prove
Where a creditor is proving, or claiming to prove, in an English insolvency, it is considered undoubted that the insolvency set-off clause will apply, regardless of whether the creditor is English or foreign, or whether the insolvent is a foreign company or a foreign individual; regardless of the governing law of either of the reciprocal claims; and regardless of the *lex situs* of the claims. This is in accordance with the principle that all matters relating to the insolvency are determined by the *lex fori*[21].

In *ex p Melbourn*[22], it was held that in an English bankruptcy a creditor, whether an alien or a British subject, can prove in accordance with the ordinary rules of English bankruptcy law any

---

15. Dicey, vol 2, pt 5.
16. Ibid., ch. 29, and also the Recognition of Trusts Act 1987.
17. Ibid., ch. 34.
18. Ibid., ch. 35.
19. Ibid., rule 175.
20. Dicey, rule 176.
21. Ibid., rules 162 and 177.
22. (1870) LR 6 Ch App 64.

debt which is due to him from the bankrupt, no matter whether the debt is governed by English law or by foreign law.

In *Re Wiskemann*[23], it was held that a foreigner proving for a foreign debt stands in the same position as does an English creditor proving for an English debt.

See also, *ex p Holthausen*[24]. This was a case involving an informal charge over property in Shanghai satisfying English security requirements, but not those of Prussia.

It would appear that similar rules apply in the case of a winding up of a company under the Companies Act 1985, i.e. the winding up, including set-off, is governed by English law[25].

Hence English law should determine such matters as to whether a debtor is excluded from proof by reason of the rule against double proof, the conversion of foreign currency claims into sterling at the insolvency date, the application of the third paragraph of the insolvency set-off clause directed against the build-up of set-offs in the twilight, and probably, the recovery by the insolvency representative without set-off of preferences, misfeasance claims, calls, the fruits of post-petition disposals and execution and the like. With regard to English jurisdiction in relation to the effect of the insolvency on antecedent transactions, such as preferences, see Dicey, rule 162.

Nevertheless, foreign laws may often be relevant, e.g. in determining whether or not a claim is invalid or is immature (for example, where the claim is affected by a foreign exchange control, a moratorium or a bankruptcy discharge) and in determining the validity of security, e.g. over foreign land, or goods in foreign parts. The ordinary rules of private international law must be resorted to to answer these questions.

Insolvency proceedings may be brought against the same debtor in more jurisdictions than one. In principle, if a creditor receives a larger set-off in foreign insolvency proceedings than he would in English insolvency proceedings, or if he effects a set-off in another jurisdiction in excess of that to which he would be entitled in the English insolvency proceedings (e.g. because of a build-up of set-off infringing the third paragraph of the insolvency set-off clause), it is

23. (1923) 92 LJ Ch 349.
24. (1874) LR 9 Ch App 722.
25. See, *Re English, Scottish and Australian Chartered Bank* [1893] 3 Ch 385, 394, CA; *Re Suidair International Airways Ltd* [1951] Ch 165, 173; *North Australian Territory Co. v Goldsbrough Malt Co.* (1899) 61 LT 716. See also, *Re Kloebe* (1884) 28 Ch D 175 (administration of deceased person's insolvent estate).

considered that the courts in England will compel him to refund the excess and bring it into hotchpot for the benefit of creditors, assuming that the courts have appropriate jurisdiction over the creditor[26].

Discharge of bankruptcy debts

An order of discharge under an English bankruptcy releases the debtor from all debts provable in the bankruptcy: Insolvency Act 1986, s. 281, subject to certain exceptions. Where an English bankruptcy discharges a debt, the debt remains discharged in an action in England, irrespective of the proper law of the debt[27]. Hence, if a loan is discharged by an English bankruptcy, the bank could not afterwards refuse to pay a deposit to the former bankrupt by purporting to set off the bank's cross-claim for the loan—the loan has been discharged and no longer exists so far as the English courts are concerned.

Foreign insolvency proceedings

An outstanding question is the position regarding set-off in England of claims which in a foreign insolvency are not available for set-off. The set-off may be prohibited in the foreign jurisdiction because, for example, the foreign jurisdiction is hostile to insolvency set-off (as in the case of France, Belgium, Luxembourg, Spain, Greece and many other Napoleonic jurisdictions), or because the set-off is a preference, or because it infringes a rule preventing set-off build-ups, or because the set-off is subject to a temporary automatic stay, as in the United States.

A foreign insolvency representative has capacity to sue in England when, for example, he is a representative of an insolvent company being wound up in the jurisdiction in which it is incorporated[28]. Hence, if the insolvency representative sues in England for a debt owed to the insolvent by a debtor in England the question will arise as to whether the debtor can set off a cross-claim owed to him by the insolvent.

If the effect of the foreign proceedings is to postpone the maturing

---

26. See *Selkrigg* v *Davies* (1814) 2 Rose 97; *ex p Wilson* (1872) LR 7 Ch 490; *Re Oriental Inland Steam Co.* (1874) LR 9 Ch App 557 (foreign proceeds of execution); *Banco de Portugal* v *Waddell* (1880) 5 App Cas 161; *Re Standard Insurance Co.* [1968] Qd S R 118 (Queensland); see the other authorities cited by Dicey, at p. 1110.
27. Dicey, rule 163 and authorities there cited.
28. See Dicey, rules 164, et seq. and 168.

of the cross-claim by virtue of a legal moratorium, the postponement will be recognised by the English courts in accordance with the general principle of English conflicts doctrine that the proper law governs discharge[29]. If the result is that the cross-claim matures after the foreign insolvency representative brings his action, the cross-claim ceases to be available for set-off in England, but without prejudice to whether it may qualify as a counterclaim if it matures in time to be pleaded in the action and if it satisfies the eligibility requirements for counterclaims.

However, if the cross-claim is governed by English law, the foreign moratorium law should be ignored since it does not arise under the governing law of the cross-claim.

In *Gibbs* v *Société Industrielle des Metaux*[30], a creditor who carried on business in England agreed under an English contract to sell copper to a debtor, a French company, carrying on business in France. The debtor refused to accept and pay for copper tendered by the creditor. Subsequently the debtor was placed under judicial liquidation in France and, as a result, its liability was by French law deemed to be discharged.
Held: The debtor was held still liable in damages to the creditor in England because the French discharge did not operate under the proper law of the contract which was English law.

Similar principles apply if the cross-claim is deemed not merely postponed by a foreign moratorium but discharged by the bankruptcy. If the foreign bankruptcy law discharges the cross-claim, it will be deemed by the English courts to be validly discharged, if the cross-claim is governed by the law of the country of the bankruptcy. If the cross-claim is discharged, the creditor has no cross-claim available for set-off.

In *Gardiner* v *Houghton*[31], a debtor was indebted to a creditor under a contract governed by the law of Victoria. The debtor was made bankrupt in Australia and obtained an order of discharge under the Australian bankruptcy law.
Held: The discharge was a good defence to an action by the creditor against the debtor in England to recover the debt.

29. Ibid., rule 187.
30. (1890) 25 QBD 399, CA.
31. (1862) 2 B & S 743.

In *Bartley* v *Hodges*[32], the debtor was indebted to a creditor under a contract governed by English law. The debtor was made bankrupt in Australia and obtained an order for discharge under the Australian bankruptcy law.

Held: The discharge was not a good defence to an action by the creditor against the debtor in England to recover the debt.

The English courts will recognise a set-off effected in foreign insolvency proceedings (provided that the foreign jurisdiction had insolvency jurisdiction in English eyes) and not permit the foreign insolvency representative to sue the creditor in England for a claim which has already been set-off. It would obviously be absurd if a foreign insolvency representative could escape his own insolvency laws by suing abroad.

In *Macfarlane* v *Norris*[33], a creditor was indorsee and holder of bill of exchange accepted by the debtor. The debtor became bankrupt in Scotland. The creditor owed the bankrupt the proceeds of sale of goods sold by the creditor on behalf of the bankrupt. Under the law of Scotland, there was an insolvency set-off. The Scots trustee sued the creditor in the English courts.

Held: Set-off. There would have been a set-off under both English and Scots law, but it seems that the court applied Scots law as the law of the place where the bankruptcy proceedings were taking place. Cockburn CJ said, at 792:

'One is shocked at the idea that the debtor who, under a Scotch bankruptcy, is entitled, by Scotch law, to have the amount of his demand allowed against the creditor by way of set-off, should, because he is sued in an English court of justice, be refused what is his undoubted right in a Scotch Court. But, on more deliberate consideration of the matter, it appears that such a set-off is a creation of statute law, while our statute law only applies to English bankruptcies, and not to those in Scotland; and perhaps it would be going too far to say that, by the equity of the English statutes, our rules would apply to give the remedy allowed by our law. I am glad to think, however, that there is no insuperable obstacle to the defendant's setting up this cross-claim. I think the effect of the plea must be taken to be that, there having been mutual credits between the defendant and the bankrupt, by the law of Scotland (whether by its statute or common law or both

32. (1861) 1 CBNS 375.
33. (1862) 2 B & S 783.

combined it is unnecessary to consider), the trustee of the estate and effects of the bankrupt is only entitled to claim, at the hands of any debtor of his estate, the amount of the balance due after credit given. It is true the pleader has adopted the form of the English plea of set-off and mutual credit; but we must take the plea as substantially amounting to this; here are mutual credits, the effect of which, by the Scotch law, is the discharge of the debtor from all excepting the balance.'

Where a foreign insolvency representative having capacity to sue in England claims a debt owing for the benefit of the foreign insolvent's estate, it is thought that the question of whether the defendant may set off a cross-claim he has against the insolvent should be governed by the law of the claim for which the foreign insolvency representatives sues in accordance with the principle suggested above in relation to independent set-off, but there is no authority for this and the principles which should govern the matter are obscure.

In this context it may be noted that the Insolvency Act 1986, s. 426(4) provides:

'The court having jurisdiction in relation to insolvency law in any part of the United Kingdom shall assist the courts having the corresponding jurisdiction in any other part of the United Kingdom or any relevant country or territory.'

Any relevant country or territory means the Channel Islands or the Isle of Man or any other country or territory designated by the Secretary of State. The latter include Australia, Canada, New Zealand, Hong Kong, Bermuda, the Cayman Islands and a number of other Commonwealth states[34].

The scope of these tentative steps in the direction of comity in international insolvencies is as yet unclear, but note the direction in s. 426(5) that the court is to have regard to private international law. A comparable provision, s. 304 of the United States Bankruptcy Code, gives the United States Bankruptcy Court in a case ancillary

---

34. See SI 1986, No. 2133. Subsection 5 provides: 'For the purposes of subsection (4) a request made to a court in any part of the United Kingdom by a court in any part of the United Kingdom or in a relevant country or territory is authority for the court to which the request is made to apply, in relation to any matter specified in the request, the insolvency law which is applicable by either court in relation to comparable matters falling within its jurisdiction.

In exercising its jurisdiction under this subsection, a court shall have regard in particular to the rules of private international law.'

to a foreign bankruptcy proceeding discretionary powers to enjoin actions in the United States with respect to property of the bankrupt debtor and to order that such property be turned over to the foreign liquidator. For an example of a set-off case where this power was employed in favour of Bahamian liquidators of a bank, see *Re Culmer*[35].

There are special rules for the mutual recognition of insolvencies within the United Kingdom as between England, Scotland and Northern Ireland[36].

Where the winding up is a solvent winding up, consideration should be given to the Brussels Convention on Jurisdiction and Enforcement of Judgments and Civil and Commercial Matters of 1968 as applied by the Civil Jurisdiction and Judgments Act 1982, which confers exclusive jurisdiction on particular courts.

---

35. 25 Bankr 621 (Bankr SDNY 1982).
36. See Dicey, Chs 30 and 31.

SOURCES OF BANK DEPOSITS: THE BANKS' RESPONSIBILITIES

Martin Karmel

The subject of this book is 'The Legal Issues of Cross-Border Banking' and it will have been noticed that the topics addressed in other papers include in their title the words 'cross-border' or 'foreign'. However, the title of this paper is merely 'Sources of Banking Deposits: The Banks' Responsibilities' and that choice of words is deliberate. The issues will be presented on the basis that in the taking of a deposit—the transaction on which the traditional banker–customer relationship is based—a bank's responsibilities, whatever they may be, are the same regardless of the presence of a cross-border or foreign element.

The general question of a bank's responsibility in respect of accepting a deposit from a new customer was raised, 'at least inferentially', in 1987 by a question posed in one of its consultation papers by the Review Committee on Banking Services Law (the Jack Committee). The wording of the question was:

> 'Should the duty on a bank to be diligent in making enquiries about a new customer, and in establishing his identity, be embodied in a code of good practice?'

One respondent to that question commented by way of reply in the following terms:

> 'Banks make enquiries about new customers seeking to open an account primarily to obtain the protection afforded to them by s. 4 of the Cheques Act 1957 and also to try and avoid customers who are likely to perpetrate frauds. A bank (or, it is submitted, any other institution that engages in the payment and collection of instruments to which s. 4 applies) would be acting in a manner contrary to its own interests if it failed to take precautionary steps on the opening of an account. It is submitted, therefore, that it is inappropriate to talk in terms of banks being under some sort of

general duty (to unidentified parties) in the circumstances to which this question relates, as surely the only duty as such on a bank is the duty of self-protection, and this hardly needs to be embodied in a code of good practice.

Nevertheless, although the banks are unable to accept the use of the word duty in the context of this question, they would not wish to argue against a generalised statement to the effect that they have a responsibility, if only to their own good name, to try to ensure that the banking system is not readily available as a cloak for criminal activities by customers. The obvious example here is the laundering of the proceeds of drug trafficking, though that is one example only, in regard to which the banks' representatives in their evidence to the House of Commons Home Affairs Committee in November 1985, expressed their views succinctly in the words "we don't want crooks on our books".

However, the essence of the point that was being made then related to the monitoring of transactions and the need on the part of banks to be alive to the possibility of misuse of the banking system for criminal purposes by an existing account-holder. The bankers were not suggesting, nor did the Select Committee recommend, that it was possible to prevent money-laundering or other misuse of the banking system by the introduction of more stringent procedures at the time of the opening of the account.

It is not accepted that there is a duty on a bank, when opening an account for a new customer, "to be diligent" in establishing his identity. This is not to say that banks will not wish to try to satisfy themselves that the customer is who he purports to be, and that they will expect some form of identification to be produced by way of confirmation, but diligence is not expected of a bank in these circumstances. Nor is a bank expected to behave inquisitorially or in the manner of an enquiry agent. There is, indeed, no means (in the absence of a foolproof national identity card system) whereby a bank, or anyone else for that matter, can "establish" a customer's identity.'

However, neither the question asked by the Jack Committee nor the rather negative reply given to it embraced the whole of the issue to be covered in this paper, which is now examined under the following two headings: a bank's responsibilities to itself, and a bank's 'responsibilities to society'. These issues will be examined separately.

A BANK'S RESPONSIBILITIES TO ITSELF

As was pointed out in the response to the Jack Committee quoted above, a bank, when taking a deposit from a new customer, is concerned to act in such a way to enable it to obtain the protection of s. 4, Cheques Act 1957[1] and also to avoid an involvement with customers who either have bad track records or are likely to be of a fraudulent disposition. Banks need to ascertain the identity of new customers and traditionally, as was shown, it was by means of personal references that the bank would try to protect itself. It may be assumed, that the requirement for references originally derived from the social and commercial practices of the 18th and 19th centuries, when it was even less of a question of what you knew rather than of whom you knew, and the possession of a bank account, which was not lightly granted by the private bankers, was regarded as a mark of respectability and social position. This perceived need for references lingered on through the first half of this century, but with the rapid growth of the banking habit in recent years (e.g. 21 million bank current accounts in 1975, 37 million in 1986), the purpose of references was becoming vaguer and the benefit to be obtained from them was recognised as dubious.

On the assumption, therefore, that banks now wish to be able to satisfy themselves about the identity of their new customers, the question is whether they have actually put themselves in a position to do so properly. In this respect the practices of one large bank (those of others may be similar) are of interest. That bank's standard practice is to undertake two forms of enquiry about a new customer, the first being a credit-reference agency search aimed at confirming the existence of the address quoted by the new customer and that he or she is registered there as a voter. The second step is to seek the production of some documentation as proof of identity.

It is submitted that neither of these two steps is really adequate. Admittedly the credit-reference agency search brings to light certain obvious kinds of attempt to deceive, but is inadequate to reveal those cases where a friend's or neighbour's address has been given, or cases where a third party's identity has been stolen. In any event, electoral registers are notorious for becoming increasingly out of date as the 'electoral year' elapses.

It may also be recognised that in the second step the so-called

---

1. Section 4 protects a collecting bank from claims in conversion, when its customer does not have title to certain instruments, notably cheques, if it acts without negligence.

proofs are largely illusory. The documents sought by the bank from a new customer include the following: driving licence, passport, state pension book, child benefit book, union card, AA membership card, etc. Apart from the passport with its photograph—and of course, not everybody is a possessor of a passport—all the other documents are as valid in the hands of a sensible thief as they are in the hands of the true owner. Consider also the ease with which these documents may be stolen and the casualness with which their loss will be treated, bearing in mind by way of example that although the banks undertake extensive advertising campaigns to warn customers to take care of their cheque cards, nevertheless a minimum of 25,000 of these cards are stolen and subsequently misused each year.

In Australia—a country whose banking laws and practices derive from and parallel those of the UK—the responsibilities of banks in the account-opening area have been more closely defined. The Australian Bankers' Association has introduced comprehensive identification procedures as well as documentation requirements for all new customers to be followed by its member banks. Even so, these are not regarded as fool-proof by the authorities in Australia and there are legislative proposals now before the Commonwealth Parliament which provide that a new account may not be operated until a prospective new customer's identification documents have been verified by means of a statutory declaration on the part of his referee. This casts the onus, at least in part, on the referees, as they will need to be more careful and be absolutely sure about the identity of the new customer for whom they have given a reference if they are to avoid the ultimate sanction of prosecution for perjury.

In some continental countries specific legal duties are imposed on banks. In Germany, for example, under Art. 154 of the Fiscal Code a credit institution is obliged 'to satisfy itself, before executing orders which are to be carried out through an account, about the identity and the address of the person having the right to operate an account'. This so-called identification check is made as a rule by the production of a valid identity card, a passport or a similar document.

Similarly in France, Art. 30 of an Edict ('Decret') of 3 October 1975 states (in translation):

'The banker must, before opening the account, verify the domicile and identity of the applicant who is required to present an official document in support. The details and references on this document shall be recorded by the banker.'

What this means in practice is that documents that are sufficiently genuine and convincing, such as a national identity card, current passport or other official document, must be presented to the bank before an account can be opened.

It is my understanding of the legal position in France that, if a bank were to fail to carry out its obligations under Art. 30, it could be exposed to liability at the suit of a third party who suffered losses as a result. What the circumstances are in which a third party could claim against a bank are not clear. It could mean no more than that the bank lost the protection of the equivalent of s. 4 of the Cheques Act, but it may go further. Certainly the dangers facing a bank in the United States which failed to be as diligent as it might be are strikingly illustrated by the following case, the details of which have been supplied by the American Bankers' Association:

A woman's identification was stolen and was used to open a new account at a financial institution. The thief began writing dud cheques. Two months after the account had been opened, the woman was stopped by a state trooper for an equipment inspection of her car. The trooper ran a computer check and discovered that there was an outstanding warrant for the woman on a bad-cheque charge. As a result, she was arrested, and spent the weekend in the county jail. A week later, she was stopped by another state trooper and it was discovered that another warrant for her arrest was outstanding on bad-cheque charges in another jurisdiction. This time she spent a day in jail.

The criminal charges pertaining to the first two arrests were dismissed in district court about two months later. However, before the woman left the district court, police officers from yet another municipality arrived and arrested her on further charges which, after investigations, were also dropped.

Six months later, the woman was interviewing for a job with the state police(!). During a routine search for past arrests and convictions, it was learned that she was wanted on bad-cheque charges in still another city. She was arrested and arraigned that day and spent the night in jail because of the discovery of yet another arrest warrant in a fifth city.

Eventually, all criminal charges against the woman were dropped because the signatures on the cashed cheques did not match hers, nor could anyone identify her in police line-ups as the person who wrote and negotiated the cheques. However, having been arrested five times on charges of writing bad cheques, she sued the bank on the grounds of negligence in that their new accounts clerk had not required sufficient identification from the person who opened a current account in her name. *The damages she was awarded by the jury amounted to half a million dollars.*

This story or, rather, this case may sound far-fetched. Certainly, some of the facts appear ludicrous but they indicate an area of potential vulnerability which has not, to the best of my knowledge, been considered here before.

There are, however, further aspects of what are described here as a bank's responsibility to itself, most significant of which is the need to maintain the confidence of depositors and the need for a bank to maintain its good name. No bank likes to be featured critically in the media, and as Montague Norman observed when he appointed the first press officer ever for the Bank of England, his job would be to keep the press out of the Bank and the Bank out of the press. A bank's reputation may suffer and it may lose its depositors' confidence for a number of reasons, not necessarily all of a prudential nature. It is apposite to mention here that one, admittedly small, bank in the United States lost 10% of its deposits within four weeks of being charged with an (unwitting) offence under the Bank Secrecy Act[2]. However, it was not the fact that it had been charged that gave rise to the flight of deposits but rather it resulted from its depositors' realisation that the offence arose out of money laundering transactions on the part of a customer of the bank who, it transpired, was a notorious pillar of the Mafia. Had the bank been more careful about the source of its deposits and been more conscious of the general application of the *noscitur a sociis* maxim, that financially unfortunate embarrassment would not have occurred.

A BANK'S 'RESPONSIBILITIES TO SOCIETY'

This part of the paper deals with the question of the conflict between a customer's entitlement to confidentiality (and a bank's correlative duty of secrecy) on the one hand, and the public interest, or the interest of the state, or the interest of society—call it what you will— on the other hand.

Potential conflict between a bank's contractual duty and the interests of the state was largely unexamined in the 60 years that followed

2. The Bank Records and Foreign Transaction Act, PubL No. 91–508.

the *Tournier* decision by the Court of Appeal in 1923[3]. Textbook writers, when commenting on this particular exception to the duty of confidentiality, had little to say other than to fall back on the suggestion advanced by Lord Chorley that it might cover the case where in time of war a customer's dealings indicated trading with the enemy[4].

So how have banks been reacting in those cases where they knew or suspected that a deposit is criminal money? Were they following the line of the Emperor Vespasian, who, when criticised for pocketing the proceeds of his new urinal tax said *'pecunia non olet'*? Or to put it another way, were they acting strictly in accordance with the following passage from the judgment of Bankes LJ in the *Tournier* case?

'A police officer goes to a banker to make an enquiry about a customer of the bank. He goes to the bank because he knows that the person about whom he wants information is a customer of the bank. The police officer is asked why he wants the information. He replies because the customer is charged with a series of frauds. Is the banker entitled to provide the information? Surely not. He acquired the information in his character of a banker.[5]'

Those of you who are bankers may know the answer to this point, but for the rest of us all we can do is to note the following extract from evidence given by bankers to the House of Commons Home Affairs Committee in November 1985:

Q. You have both referred to monitoring exercises carried out by the banks which apparently disclosed a number of suspicious cases, and I think you both said that coincidentally the police inquiries began at round about the same time. From the answers you have given today, presumably if the police had not initiated inquiries themselves, there was nothing else you could have done about it. Is that the position?

A. Not quite, but I think, as this is a public inquiry, I would not like to pursue that one any further. We have our own means.

Q. Perhaps we ought to leave it at that. I was going to ask what was the point of your monitoring in the first place.

---

3. [1924] 1 KB 461.
4. *Law of Banking*, 6th ed., 1974, p. 23.
5. At p. 474.

> Presumably there was some point, but you are not willing to elaborate on that?
>
> *A.* Not in public.

What bankers may have been doing individually on an informal, and not to be publicly disclosed basis, is one thing. How they are to equate their private duty with their public responsibility is an entirely different matter.

In the United States this problem has been addressed by means of comprehensive money laundering legislation, The Money Laundering Control Act 1986[6], which imposed substantial penalties on financial institutions and their employees for participation in the newly-created crime of money laundering.

That Act created the s. 1956 crime which is committed by any person or financial institution that knowingly participates or attempts to participate in any financial transaction which involves the proceeds of specified unlawful activity. The wording used is drawn in such terms as to make it clear that a defendant cannot plead in his defence that he thought that the property involved in the transaction represented the proceeds of a crime not covered in the list of 'specified unlawful activities'. The defendant need only know that the transaction involved the proceeds of some form of felonious activity. Moreover, this standard of knowledge required will be less than actual knowledge and will certainly include cases of wilful blindness. For example, the currency exchanger who participates in a transaction with a known drug dealer and accepts a commission far above the market rate could be convicted of the s. 1956 offence even though he did not know for sure that the currency involved in the transaction was derived from crime.

And if the s. 1956 offence is not tough enough, there is also the s. 1957 offence which appears to be knowingly to engage in, or to admit to engage in, a monetary transaction in criminally derived property of a value greater than $10,000 which is derived from specified unlawful activity. This section is, or should be, of even greater concern to banks than s. 1956, and suggests that banks should avoid participating in transactions such as accepting deposits from individuals known, or even suspected, to be engaged in specified unlawful activity.

As regards this specific point of laundering cash, the relevant United States legislation is the Bank Secrecy Act, so called because it abolishes the doctrine of banking secrecy at least in respect of cash

6. PubL No. 99–570.

transactions for amounts of $10,000 or more. For every one of these transactions a bank has to complete (unless the customer is engaged in an exempt occupation, e.g. a transport undertaking whose business is legitimately cash-based) a separate cash transaction report, identifying the parties and the destination of the cash in question. The report is then filed with the Inland Revenue service for scrutiny[7].

There have been well publicised cases of breaches by banks in the United States of their reporting obligations under this legislation and substantial fines have been imposed in respect of these breaches. However, it transpires on examination, that those breaches have been largely technical, and it remains an open question whether the Act has met with any real success and whether any serious criminals have been brought to justice as a result of its provisions. Certainly the United States Treasury has never been able to establish that the benefits that the Act was meant to bring about have matched the substantial administrative costs incurred by banks and the IRS itself in complying with its requirements.

The United Kingdom approach adopted in the Drug Trafficking Offences Act 1986, is of a subtler nature. The new offence contained in s. 24 of that Act (see Appendix on pp. 90–1)—assisting another to retain the benefit of drug trafficking—is designed to catch those who assist the trafficker and benefit from his crimes by laundering the proceeds. The offence consists of entering into, or being involved in, an arrangement the purpose of which is to facilitate the retention, control, or investment by another person of his drug trafficking proceeds; or to secure that such proceeds are used to place funds at the trafficker's disposal or to acquire property by way of investment for the trafficker's benefit. In order to safeguard those who might innocently enter into a transaction with a person who happens to be a trafficker, the prosecution must also prove that the defendant knew, or suspected, that the person with whom or on whose behalf he is dealing is, or has been, engaged in drug trafficking. As a further safeguard, it is a defence for the accused to show (on a balance of probabilities) that he did not know, or suspect, that the arrangement related to the proceeds of drug trafficking, or that the arrangement would have the effect of assisting the trafficker.

Section 24 also provides that where a person discloses to a constable a suspicion or belief that any funds or investments may be derived from, or connected with, drug trafficking, the disclosure shall not be treated as a breach of contract. This provision enables banks

---

7. 31 USC, ss. 5311–5326.

to overcome not merely the rigours of *Tournier*[8], but to go even further, to the extent of reporting the *suspicion* that a client's finances may be connected with drug trafficking; but it also covers any other person who might develop such a suspicion without actually handling the suspect funds, such as auditors, accountants and employees.

The Act also provides an exemption from the laundering offence where a person continues to handle the suspect's account after informing the police of his suspicions, or informs the police as soon as possible after the transaction[9]. Otherwise a bank might feel obliged to safeguard itself against the new offence by closing the suspected trafficker's account, possibly alerting him in the process.

CONCLUSION

Working as we do in what is now described as a financial global village, it follows that money derived from international crime is going to find its way into the global financial system through the easiest point of entry that can be found. If the account-holder has to have produced valid proof of his identity when opening an account in France or Germany, he will be unwilling to expose himself to risk by using that account for the paying in of tainted money. Likewise, he will be in difficulty in the United States under the provisions of the Money Laundering Act and will wish to bank elsewhere. So also in the United Kingdom he should be chary about exposing himself to the risk of bank officials reporting their suspicions of him, with impunity, to the police. The consequence of all this is that criminals will try to find the weakest point in the global financial system, and having found those weak points, the money will thereafter find its way, all nicely laundered, into London, New York, Paris and Frankfurt.

This is a problem that has already been considered on an international basis. As long ago as 1980 the Council of Europe concluded that '... the banking system can play a highly effective preventative role while the co-operation of the banks also assists in the repression of criminal acts by the judicial authorities and the police'[10]. The

8. [1924] 1 KB 461.
9. s. 24 (3).
10. Measures against the transfer and safeguarding of funds of criminal organisations. Recommendation Number R (80) 10. Adopted by the Committee of Ministers of the Council of Europe, 27 June 1980.

debate has been carried forward at the international level by law enforcement agencies, legislators and bank supervisors who have been considering a number of options. One option under consideration is the possibility of the adoption on an international basis of a code of conduct for the taking of deposits, for the express purpose of maintaining the integrity of, and public confidence in, institutions responsible for the transfer of payments across national borders and to prevent the utilisation of financial institutions to further illegal activity.

No details of these discussions by bank supervisors have been made public, but it is possible that what is under consideration now is a code of conduct based on the recent agreement by the member banks of the Swiss Bankers' Association, the preamble of which is in the following terms:

> '—With a view to preserving the good name of the Swiss banking community, nationally and internationally,
> —with a view to establishing rules ensuring, in the area of banking secrecy and when accepting funds, business conduct that is beyond reproach,
>
> the banks hereby contract with the Swiss Bankers' Association in its capacity as the professional body charged with safeguarding the interests and reputation of Swiss banking:
>
> (a) to verify the identity of their contracting partners and, in cases of doubt, to obtain from the contracting partner a declaration setting forth the identity of the beneficial owner to whom the assets entrusted to the bank belong;
> (b) not to provide any active assistance in the flight of capital;
> (c) not to provide any active assistance in cases of tax evasion or similar acts, by delivering incomplete or misleading attestations.'

There now seem to be enough straws in the wind to suggest:

(a) That the traditional view of a bank's responsibilities in relation to its customers and the nature of their deposits, as expressed last year by the British Bankers Association in its evidence to the Jack Committee, may be hard to maintain in the light of all the various international comparisons of which mention has been made earlier in this paper.

(b) That the traditional duty of confidence will be eroded by further statutory exceptions replicating some of the provisions of s. 24(3) of the Drug Trafficking Offences Act. Indeed, whether it be as a result of parliamentary pressure here or in consequence of recommendations by the Jack Committee or following on from some international initiatives on the part of banking supervisors, it seems likely that a bank's responsibilities to what I have described as society will before too long become more closely defined than has been the case in the past.

APPENDIX

Extract from Drug Trafficking Offences Act 1986

Offence of assisting drug traffickers

Assisting another to retain the benefit of drug trafficking

24.—(1) Subject to subsection (3) below, if a person enters into or is otherwise concerned in an arrangement whereby—
  (a) the retention or control by or on behalf of another (call him "A") of A's proceeds of drug trafficking is facilitated (whether by concealment, removal from the jurisdiction, transfer to nominees or otherwise), or
  (b) A's proceeds of drug trafficking—
      (i) are used to secure that funds are placed at A's disposal, or
      (ii) are used for A's benefit to acquire property by way of investment,
knowing or suspecting that A is a person who carries on or has carried on drug trafficking or has benefited from drug trafficking, he is guilty of an offence.

(2) In this section, references to any person's proceeds of drug trafficking include a reference to any property which in whole or in part directly or indirectly represented in his hands his proceeds of drug trafficking.

(3) Where a person discloses to a constable a suspicion or belief that any funds or investments are derived from or used in connection

with drug trafficking or any matter on which such a suspicion or belief is based—

  (a) the disclosure shall not be treated as a breach of any restriction upon the disclosure of information imposed by contract, and

  (b) if he does any act in contravention of subsection (1) above and the disclosure relates to the arrangement concerned, he does not commit an offence under this section if the disclosure is made in accordance with this paragraph, that is—

      (i) it is made before he does the act concerned, being an act done with the consent of the constable, or

      (ii) it is made after he does the act, but is made on his initiative and as soon as it is reasonable for him to make it.

(4) In proceedings against a person for an offence under this section, it is a defence to prove—

  (a) that he did not know or suspect that the arrangement related to any person's proceeds of drug trafficking, or

  (b) that he did not know or suspect that by the arrangement the retention or control by or on behalf of A of any property was facilitated or, as the case may be, that by the arrangement any property was used as mentioned in subsection (1) above, or

  (c) that—

      (i) he intended to disclose to a constable such a suspicion, belief or matter as is mentioned in subsection (3) above in relation to the arrangement, but

      (ii) there is reasonable excuse for his failure to make disclosure in accordance with subsection (3) (b) above.

(5) A person guilty of an offence under this section shall be liable—

  (a) on conviction on indictment, to imprisonment for a term not exceeding fourteen years or to a fine or to both, and

  (b) on summary conviction, to imprisonment for a term not exceeding six months or to a fine not exceeding the statutory maximum or to both.

THE FREEZING AND EXPROPRIATION OF BANK DEPOSITS

Ross Cranston

Expropriation (or nationalisation) means the taking into public ownership of property previously in private hands, with or without compensation. A bank deposit can be either directly expropriated or indirectly expropriated as the result of the expropriation of the assets of the bank where it is located. A moratorium in relation to a deposit does not go as far, but involves legal action postponing the obligation of a bank to repay. Exchange control may subject repayment to conditions, such as payment in the local currency, even if the deposit was made in a foreign currency. There may be legal issues such as constitutionality, vires or interpretation within the jurisdiction (say, state A) imposing the expropriation, moratorium or exchange control. There may be legal issues in public international law as to whether, say, state B can seek redress against state A, where the deposits expropriated belonged to citizens of only state B. The legal issue addressed here, however, is whether legal redress can be sought in the courts of state B in relation to what has occurred in state A. Legal action may be contemplated in state B because legal redress in state A is hopeless and because the head office, or another office of the deposit bank, is located in state B so that there are assets available for any judgment.

A freeze order, in relation to a bank deposit, is similar in effect to a moratorium; it postpones the obligation of the bank to repay. State B orders that certain bank deposits are not to be repaid unless, for example, a special licence is obtained. The legal issue discussed here is the extraterritorial effect of the freeze order. Granted that the order has effect in state B, will the courts of state A enforce it insofar as it purports to extend to deposits with any branch of a bank with its head office in state B, including a branch in state A?

What follows is a discussion of the rules applied by English courts to determine these issues. Beginning with the basic cases, it will be seen that while the rules are underlaid with policy considerations, their application is rather technical. By contrast, policy is more overt in the rules applied by United States courts, and some mention is made of these.

PRINCIPLES

The first relevant principle of English law is that the legal character of the relationship between banker and customer is that of debtor and creditor. The bank is the debtor of the customer, whether the customer has a current or deposit account, or has a time deposit represented by a certificate of deposit (CD)[1]. The bank is thus obliged to repay the money borrowed according to the terms of the deposit. Of course the basic debtor–creditor relationship is subject to modification between the parties.

The second principle is that the promise of the bank to repay is localised at the branch where the deposit is kept[2]. This is quite independent of whether the branch is just a branch or has a separate corporate form. The legal basis of the principle is somewhat elusive. It is going too far to say that, as a matter of law, branches of banks are always regarded as independent entities. Certainly for various purposes they are treated as such; localisation of the obligation to pay is one[3]. Inasmuch as courts have been explicit about localisation of this obligation to repay, they have put it on the basis of an implied term in the deposit contract rather than as a matter of law[4]. The origin of the principle is practical. As Atkin LJ put it on one occasion, it is at the branch where the account is kept that the precise obligation of the bank can be readily ascertained. 'A decision to the contrary would subvert banking business'[5]. Modern technology, it has been said, means that this is no longer the case[6]. However, it is questionable whether, in international banking, access of one branch to the deposit records of another branch of the same bank is any easier than was inter-bank telephonic communication within England at the time of Atkin LJ's remarks. In any event, in the common law world, including the United States, the principle is still firmly entrenched.

The second principle is subject to modification. First, there might well be an agreement to the contrary[7]. This agreement might be formal, as where the terms of a CD indicate that it is repayable

---

1. *Foley* v *Hill* (1848) 9 ER 1002.
2. The leading authority is *Joachimson* v *Swiss Bank Corporation* [1921] 3 KB 110, 127, 129–30. See also *Arab Bank Ltd* v *Barclays Bank Ltd* [1954] AC 495, 531. For the United States, *Sokoloff* v *National City Bank* (1928) 164 NE 745, 749.
3. *Libyan Arab Foreign Bank* v *Bankers Trust Company* [1987] 2 FTLR 509, 522; [1988] 1 Lloyd's Rep 259, 271; cf. *R* v *Grossman* (1981) 73 Cr App R 302.
4. *Joachimson* v *Swiss Bank Corporation*, at pp. 129–30.
5. Ibid.
6. See *Gavilanes* v *Matavosian* 475 NYS 2d 987 (1984).
7. *Richardson* v *Richardson* [1927] P 228, 232.

by any branch of the bank in the world[8]. It might be informal, as where bank officials make an oral representation that the bank as a whole, or the head office of the bank, undertakes that deposits at a branch will be repaid whatever transpires at that branch[9]. Moreover, and subject to the usual prerequisites as to the existence of a contract, modification might occur as a result of a subsequent contract between the customer and other parts of the bank, such as the head office, under which the latter agrees to repay[10].

Secondly, the bank as a whole is liable in cases of what can be called credit risk. 'If', said the Privy Council in one case, 'the manager of the St. John's branch New Brunswick refused payment, or if the branch itself were closed, the bank in London would, of course, be liable as a principal ...'[11]. The same result would follow where the deposit branch cannot operate because of physical destruction of the premises or records, or because it is financially embarrassed. The only English decision to apply this principle appears to be *Leader* v *Direction der Disconto Gesellschaft*[12]. There, the plaintiffs had an account with the Berlin office of the defendants. On 1 August 1914, when the account was in credit, they asked the bank to remit the balance. The bank declined, probably because they knew that war was imminent. War broke out on 4 August. Scrutton J held that the London branch of the bank was liable. Similarly, the Supreme Court of India held that an Indian bank could be sued in India when one of its branches in Pakistan, at which the plaintiff had a deposit, closed its doors, shortly after the partition of the sub-continent. The result might have been different, said the court, if the Pakistan government had expropriated the deposit[13].

In a leading New York case, the head office of a United States bank was held liable for failing to repay moneys deposited with its Petrograd branch. Demands were made on the customer's behalf, but the bank refused to repay. The Petrograd branch's subsequent expropriation by the Soviet government is irrelevant to the reasoning of the court, although possibly not to the outcome[14]. The same result

8. *Manas y Pineiro* v *Chase Manhattan Bank* 443 F Supp 418 (1978).
9. One explanation of *Garcia* v *Chase Manhattan Bank* 735 F2d 645 (1984).
10. The explanation of *Isaacs* v *Barclays Bank Ltd* [1943] 2 All ER 682.
11. *R* v *Lovitt* [1912] AC 212, 219.
12. (1914) 31 TLR 83. This was not questioned in later proceedings: [1915] 3 KB 154.
13. *United Commercial Bank Ltd* v *Okara Grain Buyers Syndicate Ltd* AIR 1968 SC 1115.
14. *Sokoloff* v *National City Bank of New York* (1928) 164 NE 745. The bank claimed it had effected payment on the customer's behalf, a view accepted by three of the seven judges.

was reached in *Vishipco Line* v *Chase Manhattan Bank*[15], where the defendant's Saigon branch closed its doors just prior to the American evacuation of Vietnam. The branch was subsequently expropriated. The second circuit Court of Appeals held that the branch's head office was liable. One ground was because 'the situs of the debt represented by the deposit would spring back and cling to the head office'.

To explain this second modification to the rule about localisation of the obligation to repay, there is no need to adopt misleading metaphors, as in *Vishipco*, about debts 'springing back' to the head office; nor is there any need to establish an implied term in the deposit contract by custom or usage that, in cases of credit risk, the head office is liable[16]. The legal rationale in the case of a bank with unincorporated branches is simply that the entity as a whole remains liable for debt obligations undertaken by its parts. The debt obligation is at the branch, but the action for breach of contract, when it is not fulfilled, can be brought elsewhere. Where the branch which refuses to pay is a separate corporate entity, the head office, or other parts of the bank, will probably not be liable. As a matter of company law, a holding company is not liable for the acts of its subsidiary, nor is one member of a group for the acts of another. Exceptionally the subsidiary, or a member, may have acted as agent of the holding company, or other member of the group, in accepting the deposit.

The third relevant principle of English law relates to conflicts of law. Sometimes, as with some CDs, the agreement between the bank and its customer settles the proper law of the banking contract. In the absence of agreement, it is now established that the proper law is the place of the branch where the deposit is located[17]. That would also be the situs of the debt, on the basis that that is where the debtor is[18]. These rules about the localisation of the proper law in the absence of agreement, and situs, accord with the second principle that the usual obligation of a bank is to repay at the branch where the deposit has been made. The authorities are not clear as to when

---

15. 660 F2d 854 (1981).
16. cf. *Wells Fargo Asia Ltd* v *Citibank NA* 612 F Supp 351 (1985).
17. *X AG* v *A Bank* [1983] 2 All ER 464; *Mackinnon* v *Donaldson Lufkin & Jenrette Securities Corporation* [1986] Ch 482, 494; *Libyan Arab Foreign Bank* v *Bankers Trust Company* [1987] 2 FTLR 509, 521–2; [1988] 1 Lloyd's Rep 259, 170–1. See also, *State Aided Bank of Travancore Ltd* v *Dhrit Ram* (1942) 12 Comp Cas 80 (PC).
18. *Dicey & Morris The Conflict of Laws*, 11th ed., 1987, Rule 115.

the rules about proper law of the banking contract, rather than the rules about situs of the deposit debt, are to be applied. As a matter of practice it does not matter in most cases, since they produce the same result.

Several consequences follow once the proper law of the banking contract or the situs of the debt has been identified. For example, the general rule is that a governmental act affecting a debt, such as expropriation, will be recognised as valid and effective in England, if the Act was valid and effective by the lex situs at the time it took effect[19]. The nationality of the owner is immaterial. Furthermore, if a deposit contract is unlawful by the proper law, it is invalid in England, as it is also insofar as performance of it is unlawful by the law of the country where it is to be performed[20].

Finally, there is a principle of English law that an act which would otherwise be regarded as effective under the rules of private international law just considered, should not be treated in this way if it is against public policy or the principles of international law[21]. While recognised in theory, the principle has been invoked in only very rare circumstances. It is confined to foreign laws which, being discriminatory on the grounds of race, religion or the like, constitute a grave infringement of human rights.

EXPROPRIATION

Expropriation laws in relation to bank deposits can take a variety of forms. They may purport to apply to deposits purely within the jurisdiction, or an attempt may be made to give them extraterritorial effect. They may simply expropriate assets, or they may transfer liabilities to another entity, so that a depositor can claim from that entity. Alternatively, they may be directed to a customer personally, or as a member of a particular class of customers, and not apply to all customers of the bank in that jurisdiction. Another form may not constitute a full expropriation, but do something less; for example, require that repayment by a bank be made in the local currency,

19. Ibid., rule 125.
20. Ibid., rule 184.
21. *Oppenheimer* v *Cattermole (Inspector of Taxes)* [1976] AC 249. There is another, specialised rule, that English law will not recognise a foreign law which discriminates against nationals of the country in time of war by purporting to confiscate their moveable property situated in the foreign state [1986] AC 368, 379.

rather than in the foreign currency in which the deposit was originally designated. Determining the nature of the expropriation law is, therefore, relevant to its legal effect both in its home jurisdiction and elsewhere. In England the effect of a foreign expropriation law is treated as a matter of fact, provable by expert evidence.

The simplest case of expropriation is where a customer has a deposit at a branch of a bank in the foreign jurisdiction, and the government of that jurisdiction passes a law expropriating all the assets of that branch without compensation, and without transferring the liabilities of the branch to another entity. The customer sues the head office, or another office, of the bank in England. If the situs of the deposit is in the foreign jurisdiction, English law will give effect to the expropriation law and deny the customer any relief. The general principle that English courts will recognise foreign expropriation laws was emphatically reaffirmed by the House of Lords in *Williams and Humbert* v *W and H Trademarks (Jersey) Ltd*[22], where the Spanish expropriation decrees under examination applied, in part, to share capital representing a number of Spanish banks. As Lord Templeton put it in this case, after referring to previous decisions:

> 'These authorities illustrate the principle that an English court will recognise the compulsory acquisition law of a foreign state and it will recognise the change of title to property which has come under the control of a foreign state and will recognise the consequences of that change of title. The English court will decline to consider the merits of compulsory acquisition'[23].

The general principle applies even if the foreign expropriation law has particular, as distinct from general effect, operating against a particular individual or class of persons. It also applies whether or not compensation is payable.

In *Arab Bank Ltd* v *Barclays Bank DCO*[24], the House of Lords held that the situs of the customer's current account with the Israeli branch of an English bank was in Israel, and therefore subject to Israeli legislation which vested it in the Custodian of the Property of Absentees. Consequently, the customer could not sue the head office of the bank in London to recover the credit balance. In an unreported Court of Appeal decision, *Khan* v *United Bank* (1981), it was common ground between the parties that the expropriation of

22. [1986] AC 368.
23. At p. 431.
24. [1954] AC 495.

a Pakistani branch by the new state of Bangladesh would be recognised by the English courts as valid and effective in respect of assets situated in Bangladesh. A similar result was reached in the United States decision *Perez* v *Chase Manhattan Bank*[25]. The New York Court of Appeals gave effect to a Cuban law permitting the government to close certain accounts of former officials of the previous government and to turn over the proceeds to the government. Consequently, certificates of deposit purchased with local currency could not be sued on in New York, even though no place of payment was specified in the certificates. The court said that the debt had multiple situs, but since one of these was in Cuba, effect must be given to the expropriation law.

Where bank deposits have a situs outside the jurisdiction of a foreign state, however, English law will not enforce a foreign law purporting to expropriate them. This is a particular application of the notion that English law will not enforce foreign laws which purport to have extraterritorial effect[26]. In one decision, a Spanish decree declared a former king to be guilty of high treason and seized all his property. The king had deposited securities in England with an English bank to the order of a Spanish agent. The agent claimed the securities for the benefit of the Spanish government, but the court held that the ex king was entitled to them[27]. The decision has been justified on the basis that the law of a state cannot change the title to property which is never within the jurisdiction of the state[28]. A United States case involving a bank deposit is *Republic of Iraq* v *First National City Bank*[29], where the United States Court of Appeals for the second circuit held that a New York bank account, owned by the estate of the late king of the country, was not within Iraq at the time that the government of that country purported to expropriate it, but was within New York, and therefore was not subject to the expropriation. Neither the English nor United States decisions seem acceptable on policy grounds.

As indicated, there are very rare circumstances in which English law will not recognise the effect of a foreign expropriation law even within the foreign jurisdiction. This is the category of expropriation law which constitutes a grave infringement of human rights. A Nazi law confiscating the deposits of Jews with banks in Germany would

25. 463 NYS 2d 764 (1983).
26. *Bank Voor Handel en Scheepvaart N.V.* v *Slatford* [1953] 1 QB 248.
27. *Banco de Vizcaya* v *Don Alfonso de Borbon y Austria* [1935] 1 KB 140.
28. *Williams & Humbert Ltd* v *W & H Trademarks (Jersey) Ltd* [1986] AC 368, 431.
29. 353 F2d 47 (1965), cert. denied 392 US 1027 (1966).

have fallen into this category, and would not have been recognised by an English court[30].

Finally, there is the rule that while recognising a foreign expropriation law, English law will not directly or indirectly enforce it if it constitutes a penal or revenue law. It is difficult to see how this rule could apply in the case of the expropriation of bank deposits. Say the national bank of a foreign jurisdiction in which the expropriated deposits are now vested were to institute proceedings in an English court to recover, say, related documentation then in England (bank pass books, cheque books, certificates for CDs, etc.). Is it asking an English court to enforce, albeit indirectly, a penal or revenue law? The answer must be in the negative. First, it is doubtful whether an expropriation law can ever be said to be of a penal or revenue nature. Secondly, it seems unlikely that the English action would constitute even an indirect enforcement of the foreign law. The transfer of ownership of the deposits to the national bank would have been perfected by the law of the foreign jurisdiction, and it would simply be that the English court was being asked to recognise the consequences of that transfer[31].

MORATORIA AND EXCHANGE CONTROL

If an English court will recognise the expropriation laws of a foreign jurisdiction, then a fortiori it will recognise both a moratorium, which postpones repayment of the deposit, and an exchange control law, which requires that repayment be in the local currency even though the original deposit was in a foreign currency. The leading cases on the legal effect of a moratorium involved mortgage bonds issued by a Greek bank. Since the bonds were by express term governed by English law, the English courts gave no effect to the Greek law declaring a moratorium on all obligations on the bonds[32]. As to recognition of foreign exchange laws, Upjohn J said in *Re Helbert Wagg & Co. Ltd*[33], 'In my judgment these courts must recognise the right of every foreign state to protect its economy by measures of foreign exchange control and by altering the value of its

---

30. *Oppenheimer* v *Cattermole (Inspector of Taxes)* [1976] AC 249.
31. *Williams & Humbert Ltd* v *W & H Trademarks (Jersey) Ltd* [1986] AC 368, 428, 431.
32. *National Bank of Greece and Athens SA* v *Metliss* [1958] AC 509; *Adams* v *National Bank of Greece SA* [1961] AC 255.
33. [1956] 1 Ch 323.

currency. Effect must be given to those measures where the law of the foreign state is the proper law of the contract or where the movable is situate within the territorial jurisdiction of the State'[34]. Upjohn J added the qualification, already indicated, that an English court would not recognise a law, even one having no extra-territorial effect, if it is against the usage of nations or public policy. An example he cited was of the Nazi legislation directed at the Jews.

FREEZES

What has been said should indicate the approach of an English court to an attempt by a foreign state, say A, to freeze repayment of a bank account with the London branch of a bank incorporated in A. Even if repayment is unlawful for the branch under the law of A, if the proper law of the deposit contract or the situs of the deposit is England, the freeze will not be given effect. This is precisely what was decided in *Libyan Arab Foreign Bank* v *Bankers Trust Company*[35], although the decision was complicated by arguments about the exact nature of the contract and the payment mechanisms regarding repayment of the particular deposit.

The facts of the case, in bare outline, involved the United States presidential freeze of 8 January 1986 of Libyan assets under the control, inter alia, of branches of United States banks located in the United States and abroad. There was no dispute that the freeze was effective in the United States itself and, if the freeze was effective in England, moneys deposited by the Libyan Arab Foreign Bank with the defendant bank at its London branch were subject to it. The first claim was for some US$131 million in a deposit account with the defendant's London branch. The action was in debt or alternatively in damages for non-payment after demand.

As already indicated, it is well accepted as a general rule of English law that a party is not excused from performing a contract just because it will be exposed to sanctions in another country. Performance is only excused if it becomes illegal by the proper law of the contract, or if it necessarily involves doing an act which is unlawful by the law of the place where the act has to be done[36]. The issue of proper law was complicated by the fact that there were two

34. At p. 351.
35. [1987] 2 FTLR 509; [1988] 1 Lloyd's Rep 259.
36. *Dicey & Morris The Conflict of Laws*, 11th ed., 1987, pp. 1213–25.

accounts, one in London and one in New York. In addition, after December 1980, there was a managed account arrangement, whereby Libyan Arab Foreign Bank agreed that all its payment orders on the London account should pass through New York. LAFB's argument was that there were separate contracts for each account, and that the proper law of the London account was England, because this is where the contract was. In addition, LAFB argued that if there was one contract, governing both accounts, it was governed by English law, or had two proper laws, England and New York. Bankers Trust argued that even if the proper law of the London account was England before 1980, from then there was one contract only, and its proper law was New York because of the managed account arrangement. Staughton J held that the general rule is that the proper law of a bank account is the law of the place where the account is kept. Even before this, as indicated earlier, there was authority for this proposition[37]. Staughton J intimated however, that in the modern age the principle was not inviolable. However, it still applied in this case: the actual entries on the London account were made, albeit on instructions from New York after December 1980, so at all material times the account was 'kept' in London[38].

If he had to choose between two contracts, or one contract with two proper laws after 1980, Staughton J would have chosen the latter. Here again Staughton J reasoned from basic banking law principles:

'There is high authority that branches of banks should be treated as separate from the head office. . . .

That notion, of course, has its limits. A judgment lawfully obtained in respect of the obligation of a branch would be enforceable in England against the assets of the head office. (That may not always be the case in America.) As with the theory that the premises of a diplomatic mission do not form part of the territory of the receiving state, I would say that it is *true for some purposes* that a branch office of a bank is treated as a separate entity from the head office.

This reasoning would support Mr Cresswell's argument that there were two separate contracts, in respect of the London account and the New York account. It also lends some support to the conclusion that if, as is my preferred solution, there was only one

37. See footnote 17.
38. At pp. 521, 270 respectively.

contract, it was governed in part by English law and in part by New York law'[39].

In the result, the rights and obligations of the parties in respect of the London account were governed by English law.

Later in his judgment, Staughton J returned to the managed account arrangement which required all instructions on the London account to go through New York. The relevant issue here was whether it had been terminated, for if so, it would have meant that even if the rights and obligations of the parties in respect of the London account had not been governed by English law at all times, they would have been once more on termination. Staughton J held that the plaintiffs were entitled unilaterally to determine the managed account arrangement on reasonable notice. His reasoning is important for banking law generally:

'I find nothing surprising in the notion that one party to a banking contract should be able to alter some existing arrangement unilaterally. Some terms, such as those relating to a time deposit, cannot be altered. But the ordinary customer can alter the bank's mandate, for example by revoking the authority of signatories and substituting others, or by cancelling standing orders or direct debits; he can transfer sums between current and deposit account; and he can determine his relationship with the bank entirely. So too the bank can ask the customer to take his affairs elsewhere. In this case it does not seem to me at all plausible that each party was locked into the managed account arrangement for all time unless the other agreed to its termination, or the entire banking relationship were ended. I accept Mr Cresswell's submission that the arrangement was in the nature of instructions or a mandate which the Libyan Bank could determine by notice. For that matter, I consider that Bankers Trust would also have been entitled to determine it on reasonable notice – which would have been somewhat longer than 24 hours in their case'[40].

What of the second point, that performance is excused under English law if it necessarily involves an act unlawful in the place where the act is to be done. Staughton J found it necessary to consider the

39. At pp. 522, 271 respectively.
40. At pp. 527, 277 respectively.

meaning of this principle, in particular what 'necessarily involved' meant. Drawing on the *Toprak* case[41], Staughton J concluded that just because a party to a contract had to equip himself for performance of it by an illegal act in another country did not bring him within the principle. So Bankers Trust would probably have to obtain dollar bills in New York, if it had to provide cash, but going to New York would not have been 'necessarily involved'.

The remainder of the judgment on the first claim was directed to this issue of whether payment or repayment to LAFB necessarily involved an act—an unlawful act—in New York.

The first aspect in this regard concerned what LAFB was entitled to in the way of payment and repayment. There is almost no authority on what a customer is entitled to in the way of banking services, even in the case of domestic banking[42]. LAFB argued that it could demand payment by means of cash (dollars or sterling), bankers draft, bankers payment, or a certificate of deposit. The argument was based on the premise that it is up to a debtor to find a way to pay if one or more methods are blocked. By contrast, Bankers Trust argued that it did not have to pay cash, because there was an implied term for this sort of Euromarket-transaction excluding the obligation to do so, and that all the other methods of payment suggested were additional banking services which it could, but was not obliged to, provide. In other words the Bankers Trust argument was that whatever the principles applying to ordinary banking transactions they do not apply in the Euromarket.

In this regard, Bankers Trust had strong support from leading authorities on money and commercial law. For example, Dr Mann in *The Legal Aspect of Money* takes the view that the Euromarket deals in credits. In his view payments are made, and obligations discharged, in the Euromarket through the medium of a credit to an account with another bank[43].

Notwithstanding such weighty opinion, Staughton J held that the obligation, being in monetary terms, was to be fulfilled either by the delivery of cash or by some other operation which the plaintiffs demanded and which the debtor was either obliged to, or was content to perform. Moreover, the bank would not be entitled to charge for the costs of transferring such a large sum of US dollar bills to

41. *Toprak Mahslerri Ofisi* v *Finagrain Compagnie Commercial Agricole et Financiere SA* [1979] 2 Lloyd's Rep 98.
42. At pp. 522–3, 272 respectively.
43. 4th ed., 1982, pp. 193–5.

London. In reaching his conclusion, he rejected an argument of Bankers Trust, that by implied term, LAFB had given up the right to cash.

In addition, Staughton J held that LAFB was entitled to payment in sterling if payment could not be made in dollars. Reliance was placed in particular on *Re Lines Brothers Ltd*[44]. Moreover, there was no term, express or implied, excluding LAFB's right to payment in sterling.

While LAFB could demand payment in cash, Staughton J held that it was not entitled to payment by all of the other means suggested. LAFB had relied on some charterparty cases, *The Brimnes*[45] and *Mardorf Peach*[46] that these days the commercial community regarded some instruments as being equivalent to cash. Staughton J rejected this approach: it was not correct to assume that the obligation of a bank was to make payment, and then to look to these cases to discover what payment was. In his view, the only means by which LAFB could obtain the fruits of their right to the credit balance, other than by cash, was by account transfer—by an in-house transfer, a correspondent bank transfer, or a complex account transfer through a system such as CHIPS, Fedwire, or London dollar clearing. Other methods suggested such as banker's draft, banker's payment or certificate of deposit eventually resulted in an account transfer.

POLICIES

There are various policy considerations underlying the legal conclusions examined above. At one level there is the relative position of the parties. In the case of expropriation without compensation, the depositor might lose everything if he or she cannot recover from the bank's head office. By the same token the bank will have already lost its business as a result of the expropriation of its branch, without having then to compensate depositors. On the other hand, the bank is probably in a better position to have its government put pressure on the expropriating state for compensation by comparison with the individual depositors. With moratoria or exchange control, however, the depositor suffers only from delay or by being paid in local

44. [1983] Ch 1.
45. [1973] QB 929, 948.
46. [1976] QB 835.

currency. It might be said that this is a type of sovereign risk, like currency fluctuations, which any depositor must wear, especially since they may be getting a higher rate of interest by depositing abroad. Of course, a moratorium might be indefinite, and exchange control so onerous, as to approach expropriation.

The freeze raises different issues. On the one hand the depositor has contracted with a bank in a jurisdiction other than the state imposing the freeze. It might have done so precisely to avoid the risk of a freeze. In the case of deposits in London, there is said to be the national interest in continuing its status as a readily accessible, international financial centre. On the other hand, depositors having a close connection with a state might well expect measures, such as freeze orders, to be taken by other countries, as one aspect of the foreign policy of those countries. Where the other country taking action has close connections with the United Kingdom government, it might be said that the English courts ought to support the measures taken.

None of these policy considerations are a sound basis for judicial decision-making. As is evident, they demand a detailed investigation of facts and, further, they are uncertain in their application. For example, will a state pursue a claim on behalf of its depositors against another state which has expropriated them, and will it be successful? Additionally, they might produce quite different results, in only slightly different circumstances, as illustrated by the fine line between a moratorium, which proves to be indefinite, and expropriation.

The policy consideration which does have a definite application in England, however, is foreign act of state. Within its own territory, as we have seen, the laws and acts of a foreign state are treated as fully valid. As Russell LJ said in one of the leading cases: 'This court will not enquire into the legality of acts done by a foreign government against its own subjects in respect of property situate in its own territory[47]. Whether compensation has been paid, or the nationality of persons whose property is affected, is immaterial. Contrast this with the United States doctrine of act of state, which is less clear cut in its application. While the original notion was that United States courts should respect the acts of foreign governments within their own borders, this has been overlaid with another notion that the doctrine is a means of maintaining a proper balance between the judicial and political branches of the government on matters bearing

---

47. *Princess Paley Olga* v *Weisz* [1929] 1 KB 718, 725.

on foreign matters. Deference to the executive branch of government has caused some United States courts to engage in considerable contortions as they have misread what the executive branch has intended[48].

48. Compare with *Allied Bank International* v *Banco Credito Agricola de Cartago* (1984) 23 ILM 741; 757 F2d 516 (1985).

CROSS-BORDER REGULATION OF BANKING

Brian Quinn

Introduction

The title of this paper leaves scope to deal with non-statutory regulation as well as the legal framework in which banking across borders is conducted. This seems to me to be right since the non-statutory part of the banking supervisor's work today is at least as interesting and as important as the legal framework.

The markets and products which we are trying to regulate are highly mobile, innovative and risky and the supervisor has to have a substantial degree of discretion to enable him to respond to what is going on both at home and abroad. I consider that a system of supervision based on detailed legal regulations would both stifle healthy innovation and prove ineffective, given the speed with which ideas and information travel nowadays, to say nothing of the difficulties of finding the slots in the legislative timetable necessary if the legislation is to keep pace.

The title is also helpful in the choice of the ambiguous word 'border'. I am left free to choose whether the context refers to geographical borders or borders of another kind. The borders defining the structure of financial systems both in the United Kingdom and abroad are being rather radically redrawn and I will say something about the task confronting regulators in devising arrangements which ensure that the necessary safeguards are in place whilst allowing the new financial instruments and markets to develop and operate in a way that the corporate and personal customer wants.

THE DEVELOPMENT OF THE INTERNATIONAL BANKING SYSTEM

The job of the banking supervisor in the 1960s was relatively simple and straightforward—or so it seems in retrospect[1]. National banking

---

1. For an account of United Kingdom supervision see, Edward P. M. Gardener, *UK Banking Supervision*, 1986 ed., London, Allen & Unwin.

systems were largely self-contained, and prudential risks limited by the quantitative ceilings on credit which applied in this and a number of other countries. Domestic markets were fairly well protected and competition was muted. Banks financed their domestic customers who, with a few exceptions, satisfied their financing needs from their principal banker; and this relationship changed little over very many years. Banks provided primarily deposit and loan facilities and their personal and corporate customers usually satisfied their other needs for financial services from a range of institutions. The markets served by these institutions were also largely self-contained, both domestically and internationally.

The long period of prosperity in the 1960s and early 1970s saw a rapid growth in the number of industrial and commercial companies with operations around the globe. They established places of business in many overseas countries and the banks tended to follow their customers, setting up overseas branches and subsidiaries of their own. Third-world countries came to look upon banks as their primary source of external finance and credit supplied to these countries grew very quickly.

All of this expansion was greatly assisted by the development of the eurodollar which funded the growth in banks' assets[2]. First came an international market in short-term deposits. This market then broadened, with longer maturities becoming traded and was followed by the development of markets in fixed coupon eurobonds, floating rate bonds and equity-linked instruments. As time has passed these markets have become closely linked by other innovations, notably by the technique of swapping fixed and floating interest-rate obligations or of obligations of differing maturities in different currencies. The result is a structure of interlocking markets which transcend national boundaries. We have, in effect, what amounts to a fully fledged international financial system of closely integrated markets.

Where the bankers go, regulators have to follow. The days have long since passed when the activities of bankers could be left to be regulated by the forces of competition, with the concomitant risks of bankruptcies. In these days of integrated markets and what is fast becoming a world banking system, one can no longer expect to isolate problems locally but must instead anticipate that they may have worldwide effects. Events in equity markets in October 1987 illustrate how integrated the financial world has become. Banking is considerably more integrated, and its regulation must take full

2. See generally Marcia Stigum, *The Money Market*, 1983, revised ed., Homewood, Ill., Dow Jones-Irwin.

110

account of the fact that banking is now in a very real sense beyond the bounds of any one nation and any one market.

But there is another change in financial structures taking place greatly complicating the regulator's task. Recently there has been a breakdown or dismantling of the borders between institutions which supply particular financial products in the markets both here and abroad. This is a process which had its origins in the United States with the reorganisation of the New York Stock Exchange in 1975 and the provision of banking or near-banking services and products by non-banks well placed to exploit the opportunities created by statutes having their origins in the 1930s. Closer to home, we have recently witnessed Big Bang in the United Kingdom. It is now commonplace to see financial conglomerates which offer a full range of services and products formerly supplied by separate companies and groups; and it is also fairly common to have a range of products offered by a single corporate entity.

This worldwide development has been spearheaded by banks, although more recently securities houses and even more traditional stockbrokers have developed international networks and have combined with banks to form international financial conglomerates. It has been described by commentators as deregulation. In fact, as many of us suspected, it is nothing of the kind—or rather it is only half of the story. With the formation of the new groups in the new markets the need for new methods of regulation has arisen.

STATUTORY REGULATION OF CROSS-BORDER BANKING BUSINESS

The United Kingdom Banking Acts of 1979 and 1987 both contain provisions which regulate banking business across national boundaries. Although the Acts relate to deposit-taking in the United Kingdom, they recognise the global nature of banking in a number of respects.

Both the 1979 and 1987 Acts give the Bank of England the discretion to take into account the nature and quality of overseas supervisory authorities in authorising banks from overseas to establish in the United Kingdom[3]. The 1987 Act also reflects the greater interdependence of banking and other financial markets. For example, it contains provisions which permit the Bank of England to disclose information to supervisors from other countries and in

---

3. ss. 3(5) and 9(3) respectively.

other markets[4]. The 1987 Act and the Financial Services Act 1986, both of which are essentially prudential in their objectives, also contain sections which enable HM Government to refuse entry or remove the authorisation of banks and other financial institutions from other countries if United Kingdom banks and financial companies should be subject to restrictions of a discriminatory nature in these countries[5]. The financial legislation in this country therefore contains provisions which provide part of the set of arrangements which regulate cross-border banking in both senses of the term. However, for a more complete picture one has to look more widely to both legal and non-legal constraints.

I first turn to Europe. Two key aims of the European Community are freedom of establishment and freedom to provide services by any one member state's institutions in any other member state. In this connection the First Banking Co-ordination Directive, which was passed in 1977, requires each member state to establish a system of prior authorisation of its credit institutions, sets down certain basic criteria of authorisation and effectively gives a right of establishment to institutions authorised by another member state[6]. This Directive was an important factor in the introduction of the United Kingdom Banking Act 1979, which was the first piece of United Kingdom legislation specifically directed towards the supervision of banks.

Following agreement on a programme designed to complete the internal market in Europe by 1992, a Second Banking Co-ordination Directive is now being discussed, which aims to enable a credit institution authorised in one member state to establish or provide services throughout the Community without further authorisation. The banking regulator of each member state will thereby place complete reliance on the standards of his colleagues in other member states. Recognising the existing differences in standards, some minimal harmonisation of supervisory standards will accompany the second Directive. The most important of these are directives defining the capital of credit institutions; and setting a community-wide standard capital adequacy ratio and minimum requirement. The Second Co-ordination Directive will not take effect until these vital accompanying pieces of legislation have also taken effect.

Alongside this work is a continuing programme of other proposals for greater harmonisation of supervisory systems. In 1983 a directive

---

4. s. 84(6).
5. Financial Services Act 1986, ss. 183 and 185; Banking Act 1987, s. 91.
6. Appendix 1—*First Council Directive*, see pp. 117–31.

requiring the supervision of banks on a consolidated basis was passed[7], and the European Commission has made recommendations to member states relating to the control of banks' large exposures and to deposit insurance. The Commission has ambitions to harmonise techniques of liquidity measurement and there have been extensive discussions on a possible directive covering the reorganisation and winding up of credit institutions in financial difficulties.

NON-STATUTORY REGULATION OF CROSS-BORDER BANKING BUSINESS

Supervisors must stay alert to what is going on in world financial markets and seek to respond quickly and cohesively to events of which the effects are not confined to a national banking system. This lesson was first learned in 1974 when the failure of a small domestic German bank, Herstatt Bank, caused strong ripple effects on confidence in banks in other centres, particularly in London. This brought home to banking regulators how interconnected different national banking systems had become and pointed out an urgent need for co-operation. The Committee on Banking Regulations and Supervisory Practices, a sub-committee of the G10 Governors widely known as the Cooke Committee, was formed in 1975 and work immediately started on what has become known as the Basle Concordat. This agreement, which does not have the force of law, sets out the responsibilities for the supervision of banks engaged in international business and has become the cornerstone of co-operation between national supervisors in the supervision of these banks[8].

In particular, the Concordat requires the home authority to take primary responsibility for supervising the operations of banks incorporated in its country on a worldwide basis, including the operations of overseas branches; and allocates responsibility for overseas subsidiaries jointly to the host and parent authority.

The failure of Banco Ambrosiano in 1982 led to a revision of the Concordat and, in particular, to the addition of the principle of consolidated supervision of banks' international activities. At successive international banking supervisory conferences in 1983 and 1986 in Rome and Amsterdam, over 80 countries not only agreed to adhere to the principles of the revised Concordat but also set up a

---

7. OJL 193/18 of 18 July 1983.
8. Appendix 2—*Committee on Banking Regulations and Supervisory Practices*, see pp. 133–40.

programme of work to put flesh on the bones of this agreement by agreeing on a series of detailed steps by which they could co-ordinate their supervisory activities.

The work of the Cooke Committee has taken an interesting turn more recently which recognises quite explicitly the global nature of the banking markets. Whereas the Concordat confined itself to general principles and leaves the particulars of implementation to each individual supervisory authority, the member countries of the Committee are now working to achieve uniformity in the measurement and application of rules governing the capital adequacy of banks which operate internationally from the G10 countries. Work on this matter is well advanced[9]. This is an important initiative and should make the world a safer place financially and reduce some of the more pronounced inequities in competition between banks from the different countries involved. Similar efforts are being made in the European Community to achieve a common solvency ratio for EC member banks. With a large degree of common membership of both G10 and the European Community it is important to try to ensure that these two exercises go forward in parallel; and as you might imagine, this demands much patience and hard work. However, we are hopeful that the regimes which emerge from both sources are at least compatible and possibly identical in most important respects.

The Cooke Committee now meets regularly four times a year, seeking to identify international banking developments which may contain the seeds of future problems and to work on the appropriate responses. This is unsung private work, founded on a free exchange of views. One of its less well publicised exercises was the common effort made in G10 countries to improve the capital adequacy of international banks during the early 1980s and resulting in a material improvement in the capital ratios of the principal international banks in several G10 countries.

Although the Basle Committee is the best known of the original supervisory groupings, its example has spread and there are now similar groupings from other areas which have regular contracts with the Cooke Committee. There are now groupings in the Far East, the Middle East, South America, the Caribbean, the Nordic countries and the principal offshore financial centres. These are usually fairly informal groups but they do enable supervisors to get to know each

9. The G10 Governors have now agreed that the Committee's proposals on capital adequacy should be implemented by 1992. National regulators are publishing their own regulations within the framework of the G10 agreement.

other and thereby short circuit the otherwise bureaucratic procedures in the event of a problem in an international bank.

THE REGULATION OF BUSINESS ACROSS FINANCIAL BORDERS

The task of devising statutory and non-statutory arrangements for the regulation of activities in the newly structured financial markets is posing new challenges for regulators used to dealing largely with single-function institutions. The first step—to put in place systems of efficient and effective supervision within individual countries— has posed awkward practical problems. The Financial Services Act 1976, the Banking Act 1987 and the Insurance Companies Act 1980 in the United Kingdom each places responsibility on a separate supervisory authority for protecting the interests of investors, depositors and insured parties, respectively. However, with all of these functions frequently being conducted within a single group, there is a clear and worrying potential for either supervisory overlap or underlap. The statutes do not permit any of the supervisors to delegate its authority and much work has therefore been going on to ensure that the regulatory arrangements both observe the legal imperatives and avoid a bureaucratic nightmare.

In the pursuit of these objectives the Bank of England and the Securities and Investment Board recently published a joint memorandum of understanding allocating responsibility for supervising institutions engaging in activities covered by more than one regulatory statute[10]. It is, I think, important to stress the need for a workable and efficient solution to these problems. London can maintain its position as a principal international financial centre along with Tokyo and New York only if participants can be clear what the statutory and other regulatory requirements are, and without incurring excessive costs in meeting these requirements.

Already supervisors are turning their attentions to the even more complicated task of ensuring that the regulators of both banks and securities companies in different countries are aware of what is going on in one another's markets and, more difficult still, can effectively regulate the growing body of institutions each of which supplies all of the relevant products in the global financial marketplace.

The need for co-operation of this kind can hardly be gainsaid. The events of October 1987 have shown that the national markets in

10. Appendix 3—*Memorandum of Understanding*, see pp. 141–5.

listed equities are highly interconnected. It became quite clear that the simultaneous collapse in the stock exchanges of the principal countries owed a great deal to the fact that the investors in these markets take a global view of their position and that sentiment and confidence were affected much more by events in each other's markets than by what was going on in the domestic economy. Banking supervisors watched these developments with great interest and some apprehension since many of the institutions they supervise were either directly involved or had substantial exposures to companies which were. They, as much as the securities regulators, looked closely at the lessons of this episode.

CONCLUSION

In the last 20 years there has been a marked change in the nature and scope of the responsibilities of the banking regulator. As world trade and commerce have expanded, both businesses and the financial institutions which serve them, have come increasingly to regard the world marketplace as their natural habitat. Most regulatory regimes derive naturally from their domestic systems and are based on legal frameworks and accounting conventions which differ significantly from country to country. National legislators are busier than ever before and their timetables are crowded. The financial markets themselves are constantly changing under the stimulus of keen competition. For all of these reasons, for cross-border regulation to be effective it is important that the relevant country statutes and EC Directives give the supervisors sufficient flexibility to respond quickly to what is happening in markets around the world.

With the liberalisation of financial systems in many of the principal developed countries, the regulation of activities across both national and international borders presents an even greater challenge and the time is probably still some way off when we may be able to point to a blueprint which provides for the regulation of the activities of all financial companies which operate across the world. Indeed, such a blueprint may never be produced. In the meantime, financial supervisors of all kinds are working and talking together to try to ensure that business can be conducted in the way which meets the requirements of consumers of financial services without neglecting the danger that undue risks may be run. There is work enough for all of us, lawyers, academicians and supervisors, for some time ahead.

Appendix 1—FIRST COUNCIL DIRECTIVE
OF 12 DECEMBER 1977 ON THE COORDINATION OF LAWS, REGULATIONS AND ADMINISTRATIVE PROVISIONS RELATING TO THE TAKING UP AND PURSUIT OF THE BUSINESS OF CREDIT INSTITUTIONS

(77/780/EEC)

The Council of the European Communities

Having regard to the Treaty establishing the European Economic Community, and in particular Article 57 thereof,

Having regard to the proposal from the Commission,

Having regard to the opinion of the European Parliament,[1]

Having regard to the opinion of the Economic and Social Committee,[2]

Whereas, pursuant to the Treaty, any discriminatory treatment with regard to establishment and to the provision of services, based either on nationality or on the fact that an undertaking is not established in the Member States where the services are provided, is prohibited from the end of the transitional period;

Whereas, in order to make it easier to take up and pursue the business of credit institutions, it is necessary to eliminate the most obstructive differences between the laws of the Member States as regards the rules to which these institutions are subject;

Whereas, however, given the extent of these differences, the conditions required for a common market for credit institutions cannot be created by means of a single Directive; whereas it is therefore necessary to proceed by successive stages; whereas the result of this process should be to provide for overall supervision of a credit institution operating in several Member States by the competent authorities in the Member State where it has its head office, in

1. O.J. No. C128, 9.6.1975, p. 25.
2. O.J. No. C263, 17.11.1975, p. 25.

consultation, as appropriate, with the competent authorities of the other Member States concerned;

Whereas measures to coordinate credit institutions must, both in order to protect savings and to create equal conditions of competition between these institutions, apply to all of them; whereas due regard must be had, where applicable, to the objective differences in their statutes and their proper aims as laid down by national laws;

Whereas the scope of those measures should therefore be as broad as possible, covering all institutions whose business is to receive repayable funds from the public whether in the form of deposits or in other forms such as the continuing issue of bonds and other comparable securities and to grant credits for their own account; whereas exceptions must be provided for in the case of certain credit institutions to which this Directive cannot apply;

Whereas the provisions of this Directive shall not prejudice the application of national laws which provide for special supplementary authorizations permitting credit institutions to carry on specific activities or undertake specific kinds of operations;

Whereas the same system of supervision cannot always be applied to all types of credit institution; whereas provision should therefore be made for application of this Directive to be deferred in the case of certain groups or types of credit institutions to which its immediate application might cause technical problems; whereas more specific provisions for such institutions may prove necessary in the future; whereas these specific provisions should nonetheless be based on a number of common principles;

Whereas the eventual aim is to introduce uniform authorization requirements throughout the Community for comparable types of credit institution; whereas at the initial stage it is necessary, however, to specify only certain minimum requirements to be imposed by all Member States;

Whereas this aim can be achieved only if the particularly wide discretionary powers which certain supervisory authorities have for authorizing credit establishments are progressively reduced; whereas the requirement that a programme of operations must be produced should therefore be seen merely as a factor enabling the competent authorities to decide on the basis of more precise information using objective criteria;

Whereas the purpose of coordination is to achieve a system whereby credit institutions having their head office in one of the Member States are exempt from any national authorization requirement when setting up branches in other Member States;

Whereas a measure of flexibility may nonetheless be possible in the initial stage as regards the requirements on the legal form of credit institutions and the protection of banking names;

Whereas equivalent financial requirements for credit institutions will be necessary to ensure similar safeguards for savers and fair conditions of competition between comparable groups of credit institutions; whereas, pending further coordination, appropriate structural ratios should be formulated that will make it possible within the framework of cooperation between national authorities to observe, in accordance with standard methods, the position of comparable types of credit institutions; whereas this procedure should help to bring about the gradual approximation of the systems of coefficients established and applied by the Member States; whereas it is necessary, however, to make a distinction between coefficients intended to ensure the sound management of credit institutions and those established for the purposes of economic and monetary policy; whereas, for the purpose of formulating structural ratios and of more general cooperation between supervisory authorities, standardization of the layout of credit institutions' accounts will have to begin as soon as possible;

Whereas the rules governing branches of credit institutions having their head office outside the Community should be analogous in all Member States; whereas it is important at the present time to provide that such rules may not be more favourable than those for branches of institutions from another Member State; whereas it should be specified that the Community may conclude agreements with third countries providing for the application of rules which accord such branches the same treatment throughout its territory, account being taken of the principle of reciprocity;

Whereas the examination of problems connected with matters covered by Council Directives on the business of credit institutions requires cooperation between the competent authorities and the Commission within an Advisory Committee, particularly when conducted with a view to closer coordination;

Whereas the establishment of an Advisory Committee of the competent authorities of the Member States does not rule out other forms of cooperation between authorities which supervise the taking

119

up and pursuit of the business of credit institutions and, in particular, cooperation within the Contact Committee set up between the banking supervisory authorities.

Has adopted this directive:

Title I—Definitions and Scope

Article 1
For the purposes of this Directive:
— 'credit institution' means an undertaking whose business is to receive deposits or other repayable funds from the public and to grant credits for its own account,
— 'authorization' means an instrument issued in any form by the authorities by which the right to carry on the business of a credit institution is granted,
— 'branch' means a place of business which forms a legally dependent part of a credit institution and which conducts directly all or some of the operations inherent in the business of credit institutions; any number of branches set up in the same Member State by a credit institution having its head office in another Member State shall be regarded as a single branch, without prejudice to Article 4(1),
— 'own funds' means the credit institution's own capital, including items which may be treated as capital under national rules.

Article 2
1. This Directive shall apply to the taking up and pursuit of the business of credit institutions.
2. It shall not apply to:
— the central banks of Member States,
— post office giro institutions,
— in Belgium, the communal savings banks ('caisses d'épargne communales—gemeentelijke spaarkassen'), the 'Institut de Réescompte et de Garantie—Herdiscontering- en Waarborginstituut', the 'Société nationale d'Investissement—Nationale Investeringsmaatschappij', the regional development companies ('sociétés de développement régional—gewestelijke ontwikkelingsmaatschappijen'), the 'Société nationale du Logement—Nationale Maatschappij voor de Huisvesting' and its authorized companies and the 'Société nationale terrienne—Nationale Landmaatschappij' and its authorized companies,

— in Denmark, the 'Dansk Eksportfinansieringsfond' and 'Danmarks Skibskreditfond',
— in Germany, the 'Kreditanstalt für Wiederaufbau', undertakings which are recognized under the 'Wohnungsgemeinnützigkeitsgesetz' (non-profit housing law) as bodies of state housing policy and are not mainly engaged in banking transactions and undertakings recognized under that law as non-profit housing undertakings,
[— in Greece:

τῆς 'Ελληνικῆς Τραπέζης Βιομηχανικῆς
Αναπτύξεως, τοῦ Ταμείου Παρακαταθηκῶν καί
Δανείων, τῆς Τραπέζης 'Υποθηκῶν, τῶν
Ταχυδρομικῶν Ταμιευτηρίων καί τῆς 'Ελληνικαί
'Εξαγωγαί Α.Ε.,]

— in France, the 'Caisse des Dépôts et Consignations', the 'Crédit Foncier' and the 'Crédit National',
— in Ireland, credit unions,
— in Italy, the 'Cassa Depositi e Prestiti',
— in the Netherlands, the 'NV Export-Financieringsmaatschappij', the 'Netherlandse Financieringsmaatschappij voor Ontwikkelingslanden NV', the 'Nederlandse Investeringsbank voor Ontwikkelingsladen NV', the 'Nationale Investeringsbank NV', the 'NV Bank van Nederlandse Gemeenten', the 'Nederlandse Waterschapsbank NV', the 'Financieringsmaatschappij Industrieel Garantiefonds Amsterdam NV', the 'Financieringsmaatschappij Industrieel Garantiefonds 's-Gravenhage NV', the 'NV Noordelijke Ontwikkelings Maatschappij', the 'NV Industriebank Limburgs Instituut voor ontwikkeling en financiering' and the 'Overijsselse Ontwikkelingsmaatschappij NV',
— in the United Kingdom, the National Savings Bank, the Commonwealth Development Finance Company Ltd, the Agricultural Mortgage Corporation Ltd, the Scottish Agricultural Securities Corporation Ltd, the Crown Agents for overseas governments and administrations, credit unions, and municipal banks.

3. The Council, acting on a proposal from the Commission, which, for this purpose, shall consult the Committee referred to in Article 11 (hereinafter referred to as 'the Advisory Committee') shall decide on any amendments to the list in paragraph 2.

4.(a) Credit institutions existing in the same Member State at the time of the notification of this Directive and permanently affiliated at that time to a central body which supervises them and which is established in that same Member State, may be exempted from the requirements listed in the first, second and third indents of the first subparagraph of Article 3(2), the second subparagraph of Article 3(2), Article 3(4) and Article 6, if, no later than the date when the national authorities take the measures necessary to translate this Directive into national law, that law provides that:

— the commitments of the central body and affiliated institutions are joint and several liabilities or the commitments of its affiliated institutions are entirely guaranteed by the central body,

— the solvency and liquidity of the central body and of all the affiliated institutions are monitored as a whole on the basis of consolidated accounts,

— the management of the central body is empowered to issue instructions to the management of the affiliated institutions.

(b) Credit institutions operating locally which are affiliated, subsequent to notification of this Directive, to a central body within the meaning of subparagraph (a) may benefit from the conditions laid down in subparagraph (a) if they constitute normal additions to the network belonging to that central body.

(c) In the case of credit institutions other than those which are set up in areas newly reclaimed from the sea or have resulted from scission or mergers of existing institutions dependent or answerable to the central body, the Council, acting on a proposal from the Commission, which shall, for this purpose, consult the Advisory Committee, may lay down additional rules for the application of subparagraph (b) including the repeal of exemptions provided for in subparagraph (a), where it is of the opinion that the affiliation of new institutions benefiting from the arrangements laid down in subparagraph (b) might have an adverse effect on competition. The Council shall decide by a qualified majority.

5. Member States may defer in whole or in part the application of this Directive to certain types or groups of credit institutions where such immediate application would cause technical problems which cannot be overcome in the short-term. The problems may result either from the fact that these institutions are subject to supervision by an authority different from that normally responsible for the supervision of banks, or from the fact that they are subject to a special system of supervision. In any event, such deferment cannot be justified by the public law statutes, by the smallness of size or by the limited scope of activity of the particular institutions concerned.

Deferment can apply only to groups or types of institutions already existing at the time of notification of this Directive.

6. Pursuant to paragraph 5, a Member State may decide to defer application of this Directive for a maximum period of five years from the notification thereof and, after consulting the Advisory Committee may extend deferment once only for a maximum period of three years.

The Member State shall inform the Commission of its decision and the reasons therefor not later than six months following the notification of this Directive. It shall also notify the Commission of any extension or repeal of this decision. The Commission shall publish any decision regarding deferment in the *Official Journal of the European Communities*.

Not later than seven years following the notification of this Directive, the Commission shall, after consulting the Advisory Committee, submit a report to the Council on the situation regarding deferment. Where appropriate, the Commission shall submit to the Council, not later than six months following the submission of its report, proposals for either the inclusion of the institutions in question in the list in paragraph 2 or for the authorization of a further extension of deferment. The Council shall act on these proposals not later than six months after their submission.

Title II—Credit Institutions Having their Head Office in a Member State and their Branches in Other Member States

Article 3

1. Member States shall require credit institutions subject to this Directive to obtain authorization before commencing their activities. They shall lay down the requirements for such authorization subject to paragraphs 2, 3 and 4 and notify them to both the Commission and the Advisory Committee.

2. Without prejudice to other conditions of general application laid down by national laws, the competent authorities shall grant authorization only when the following conditions are complied with:
— the credit institution must possess separate own funds,
— the credit institution must possess adequate minimum own funds,
— there shall be at least two persons who effectively direct the business of the credit institution.

Moreover, the authorities concerned shall not grant authorization if the persons referred to in the third indent of the first subparagraph are not of sufficiently good repute or lack sufficient experience to perform such duties.

3.(a) The provisions referred to in paragraphs 1 and 2 may not require the application for authorization to be examined in terms of the economic needs of the market.

(b) Where the laws, regulations or administrative provisions of a Member State provide, at the time of notification of the present Directive, that the economic needs of the market shall be a condition of authorization and where technical or structural difficulties in its banking system do not allow it to give up the criterion within the period laid down in Article 14(1), the State in question may continue to apply the criterion for a period of seven years from notification.

It shall notify its decision and the reasons therefor to the Commission within six months of notification.

(c) Within six years of the notification of this Directive the Commission shall submit to the Council, after consulting the Advisory Committee, a report on the application of the criterion of economic need. If appropriate, the Commission shall submit to the Council proposals to terminate the application of that criterion. The period referred to in subparagraph (b) shall be extended for one further period of five years, unless, in the meantime, the Council, acting unanimously on proposals from the Commission, adopts a Decision to terminate the application of that criterion.

(d) The criterion of economic need shall be applied only on the basis of general predetermined criteria, published and notified to both the Commission and the Advisory Committee and aimed at promoting:

— security of savings,
— higher productivity in the banking system,
— greater uniformity of competition between the various banking networks,
— a broader range of banking services in relation to population and economic activity.

Specification of the above objectives shall be determined within the Advisory Committee, which shall begin its work as from its initial meetings.

4. Member States shall also require applications for authorization to be accompanied by a programme of operations setting out *inter alia* the types of business envisaged and the structural organization of the institution.

5. The Advisory Committee shall examine the content given by the competent authorities to requirements listed in paragraph 2,

any other requirements which the Member States apply and the information which must be included in the programme of operations, and shall, where appropriate, make suggestions to the Commission with a view to a more detailed coordination.

6. Reasons shall be given whenever an authorization is refused and the applicant shall be notified thereof within six months of receipt of the application or, should the latter be incomplete, within six months of the applicant's sending the information required for the decision. A decision shall, in any case, be taken within 12 months of the receipt of the application.

7. Every authorization shall be notified to the Commission. Each credit institution shall be entered in a list which the Commission shall publish in the *Official Journal of the European Communities* and shall keep up to date.

Article 4

1. Member States may make the commencement of business in their territory by branches of credit institutions covered by this Directive which have their head office in another Member State subject to authorization according to the law and procedure applicable to credit institutions established on their territory.

2. However, authorization may not be refused to a branch of a credit institution on the sole ground that it is established in another Member State in a legal form which is not allowed in the case of a credit institution carrying out similar activities in the host country. This provision shall not apply, however, to credit institutions which possess no separate own funds.

3. The competent authorities shall inform the Commission of any authorizations which they grant to the branches referred to in paragraph 1.

4. This Article shall not affect the rules applied by Member States to branches set up on their territory by credit institutions which have their head office there. Notwithstanding the second part of the third indent of Article 1, the laws of Member States requiring a separate authorization for each branch of a credit institution having its head office in their territory shall apply equally to the branches of credit institutions the head offices of which are in other Member States.

Article 5

For the purpose of exercising their activities, credit institutions to which this Directive applies may, notwithstanding any provisions concerning the use of the words 'bank', 'saving bank' or other banking names which may exist in the host Member State, use throughout the territory of the Community the same name as they use in the Member States in which their head office is situated. In the event of there being any danger of confusion, the host Member State may, for the purposes of clarification, require that the name be accompanied by certain explanatory particulars.

Article 6

1. Pending subsequent coordination, the competent authorities shall, for the purposes of observation and, if necessary, in addition to such coefficients as may be applied by them, establish ratios between the various assets and/or liabilities of credit institutions with a view to monitoring their solvency and liquidity and the other measures which may serve to ensure that savings are protected.

To this end, the Advisory Committee shall decide on the content of the various factors of the observation ratios referred to in the first subparagraph and lay down the method to be applied in calculating them.

Where appropriate, the Advisory Committee shall be guided by technical consultations between the supervisory authorities of the categories of institutions concerned.

2. The observation ratios established in pursuance of paragraph 1 shall be calculated at least every six months.

3. The Advisory Committee shall examine the results of analyses carried out by the supervisory authorities referred to in the third subparagraph of paragraph 1 on the basis of the calculations referred to in paragraph 2.

4. The Advisory Committee may make suggestions to the Commission with a view to coordinating the coefficients applicable in the Member States.

Article 7

1. The competent authorities of the Member States concerned shall collaborate closely in order to supervise the activities of credit institutions operating, in particular by having established branches there, in one or more Member States other than that in which their head offices are situated. They shall supply one another with all information concerning the management and ownership of such credit institutions that is likely to facilitate their supervision and the examination of the conditions for their authorization and all

information likely to facilitate the monitoring of their liquidity and solvency.

2. The competent authorities may also, for the purposes and within the meaning of Article 6, lay down ratios applicable to the branches referred to in this Article by reference to the factors laid down in Article 6.

3. The Advisory Committee shall take account of the adjustments necessitated by the specific situation of the branches in relation to national regulations.

Article 8

1. The competent authorities may withdraw the authorization issued to a credit institution subject to this Directive or to a branch authorized under Article 4 only where such an institution or branch:

(a) does not make use of the authorization within 12 months, expressly renounces the authorization or has ceased to engage in business for more than six months, if the Member State concerned has made no provision for the authorization to lapse in such cases;

(b) has obtained the authorization through false statements or any other irregular means;

(c) no longer fulfils the conditions under which authorization was granted, with the exception of those in respect of own funds;

(d) no longer possesses sufficient own funds or can no longer be relied upon to fulfil its obligations towards its creditors, and in particular no longer provides security for the assets entrusted to it;

(e) falls within one of the other cases where national law provides for withdrawal of authorization.

2. In addition, the authorization issued to a branch under Article 4 shall be withdrawn if the competent authority of the country in which the credit institution which established the branch has its head office has withdrawn authorization from that institution.

3. Member States which grant the authorizations referred to in Articles 3(1) and 4(1) only if, economically, the market situation requires it may not invoke the disappearance of such a need as grounds for withdrawing such authorizations.

4. Before withdrawal from a branch of an authorization granted under Article 4, the competent authority of the Member State in

which its head office is situated shall be consulted. Where immediate action is called for, notification may take the place of such consultation. The same procedure shall be followed, by analogy, in cases of withdrawal of authorization from a credit institution which has branches in other Member States.

5. Reasons must be given for any withdrawal of authorization and those concerned informed thereof; such withdrawal shall be notified to the Commission.

Title III—Branches of Credit Institutions Having their Head Offices Outside the Community

Article 9

1. Member States shall not apply to branches of credit institutions having their head office outside the Community, when commencing or carrying on their business, provisions which result in more favourable treatment than those accorded to branches of credit institutions having their head office in the Community.

2. The competent authorities shall notify the Commission and the Advisory Committee of all authorizations for branches granted to credit institutions having their head office outside the Community.

3. Without prejudice to paragraph 1, the Community may, through agreements concluded in accordance with the Treaty with one or more third countries, agree to apply provisions which, on the basis of the principle of reciprocity, accord to branches of a credit institution having its head office outside the Community identical treatment throughout the territory of the Community.

Title IV—General and Transitional Provisions

Article 10

1. Credit institutions subject to this Directive, which took up their business in accordance with the provisions of the Member States in which they have their head offices before the entry into force of the provisions implementing this Directive shall be deemed to be authorized. They shall be subject to the provisions of this Directive concerning the carrying on of the business of credit institutions and to the requirements set out in the first and third indents of the first subparagraph and in the second subparagraph of Article 3(2).

Member States may allow credit institutions which at the time of notification of this Directive do not comply with the requirement laid down in the third indent of the first subparagraph of Article 3(2), no more than five years in which to do so.

Member States may decide that undertakings which do not fulfil the requirements set out in the first indent of the first subparagraph of Article 3(2) and which are in existence at the time this Directive enters into force may continue to carry on their business. They may exempt such undertakings from complying with the requirement contained in the third indent of the first subparagraph of Article 3(2).

2. All the credit institutions referred to in paragraph 1 shall be given in the list referred to in Article 3(7).

3. If a credit institution deemed to be authorized under paragraph 1 has not undergone any authorization procedure prior to commencing business, a prohibition on the carrying on of its business shall take the place of withdrawal of authorization.

Subject to the first subparagraph, Article 8 shall apply by analogy.

4. By way of derogation from paragraph 1, credit institutions established in a Member State without having undergone an authorization procedure in that Member State prior to commencing business may be required to obtain authorization from the competent authorities of the Member State concerned in accordance with the provisions implementing this Directive. Such institutions may be required to comply with the requirement in the second indent of Article 3(2) and with such other conditions of general application as may be laid down by the Member State concerned.

Article 11

1. An 'Advisory Committee of the Competent Authorities of the Member States of the European Economic Community' shall be set up alongside the Commission.

2. The tasks of the Advisory Committee shall be to assist the Commission in ensuring the proper implementation of both this Directive and Council Directive 73/183/EEC of 28 June 1973 on the abolition of restrictions on freedom of establishment and freedom to provide services in respect of self-employed activities of banks and other financial institutions[3] in so far as it relates to credit institutions. Further it shall carry out the other tasks prescribed by this Directive and shall assist the Commission in the preparation of new proposals to the Council concerning further coordination in the sphere of credit institutions.

3. O.J. No. L194, 16.7.1973, p. 1.

3. The Advisory Committee shall not concern itself with concrete problems relating to individual credit institutions.

4. The Advisory Committee shall be composed of not more than three representatives from each Member State and from the Commission. These representatives may be accompanied by advisers from time and subject to the prior agreement of the Committee. The Committee may also invite qualified persons and experts to participate in its meetings. The secretariat shall be provided by the Commission.

5. The first meeting of the Advisory Committee shall be convened by the Commission under the chairmanship of one of its representatives. The Advisory Committee shall then adopt its rules of procedure and shall elect a chairman from among the representatives of Member States. Thereafter it shall meet at regular intervals and whenever the situation demands. The Commission may ask the Committee to hold an emergency meeting if it considers that the situation so requires.

6. The Advisory Committee's discussions and the outcome thereof shall be confidential except when the Committee decides otherwise.

Article 12

1. Member States shall ensure that all persons now or in the past employed by the competent authorities are bound by the obligation of professional secrecy. This means that any confidential information which they may receive in the course of their duties may not be divulged to any person or authority except by virtue of provisions laid down by law.

2. Paragraph 1 shall not, however, preclude communications between the competent authorities of the various Member States, as provided for in this Directive. Information thus exchanged shall be covered by the obligation of professional secrecy applying to the persons now or in the past employed by the competent authorities receiving the information.

3. Without prejudice to cases covered by criminal law, the authorities receiving such information shall use it only to examine the conditions for the taking up and pursuit of the business of credit institutions, to facilitate monitoring of the liquidity and solvency of these institutions or when the decisions of the competent authority are the subject of an administrative appeal or in court proceedings initiated pursuant to Article 13.

Article 13

Member States shall ensure that decisions taken in respect of a credit institution in pursuance of laws, regulations and administrative provisions adopted in accordance with this Directive may be subject to the right to apply to the courts. The same shall apply where no decision is taken within six months of its submission in respect of an application for authorization, which contains all the information required under the provisions in force.

Title V—Final Provisions

Article 14

1. Member States shall bring into force the measures necessary to comply with this Directive within 24 months of its notification and shall forthwith inform the Commission thereof.

2. As from the notification of this Directive, Member States shall communicate to the Commission the texts of the main laws, regulations and administrative provisions which they adopt in the field covered by this Directive.

Article 15

This Directive is addressed to the Member States.

Done at Brussels, 12 December 1977.

For the Council
The President
A. HUMBLET

Appendix 2—COMMITTEE ON BANKING REGULATIONS AND SUPERVISORY PRACTICES: THE 'BASLE CONCORDAT'

Principles for the supervision of banks' foreign establishments

This report sets out certain principles which the Committee believes should govern the supervision of banks' foreign establishments by parent and host authorities. It replaces the 1975 Concordat and reformulates some of its provisions, most particularly to take account of the subsequent acceptance by the governors of the principle that banking supervisory authorities cannot be fully satisfied about the soundness of individual banks unless they can examine the totality of each bank's business worldwide through the technique of consolidation.

The report deals exclusively with the responsibilities of banking supervisory authorities for monitoring the prudential conduct and soundness of the business of banks' foreign establishments. It does not address itself to lender-of-last-resort aspects of the rôle of central banks.

The principles set out in the report are not necessarily embodied in the laws of the countries represented on the committee. Rather they are recommended guidelines of best practices in this area, which all members have undertaken to work towards implementing, according to the means available to them.

Adequate supervision of banks' foreign establishments calls not only for an appropriate allocation of responsibilities between parent and host supervisory authorities but also for contact and co-operation between them. It has been, and remains, one of the committee's principal purposes to foster such co-operation both among its member countries and more widely. The committee has been encouraged by the like-minded approach of other groups of supervisors and it hopes to continue to strengthen its relationships with these other groups and to develop new ones. It strongly commends the principles set out in this report as being of general validity for all those who are responsible for the supervision of banks which conduct international business and hopes that they will be progressively accepted and implemented by supervisors worldwide.

Where situations arise which do not appear to be covered by the principles set out in this report, parent and host authorities should explore together ways of ensuring that adequate supervision of banks' foreign establishments is effected.

1. Types of banks' foreign establishments

Banks operating internationally may have interests in the following types of foreign banking establishment:

(a) *Branches*—operating entities which do not have a separate legal status and are thus integral parts of the foreign parent bank;

(b) *Subsidiaries*—legally independent institutions wholly-owned or majority-owned by a bank which is incorporated in a country other than that of the subsidiary;

(c) *Joint ventures or Consortia*—legally independent institutions incorporated in the country where their principal operations are conducted and controlled by two or more parent institutions, most of which are usually foreign and not all of which are necessarily banks. While the pattern of shareholdings may give effective control to one parent institution, with others in a minority, joint ventures are, most typically, owned by a collection of minority shareholders.

In addition, the structure of international banking groups may derive from an ultimate holding company which is not itself a bank. Such a holding company can be an industrial or commercial company, or a company the majority of whose assets consists of shares in banks. These groups may also include intermediate non-bank holding companies or other non-banking companies.

Banks may also have minority participations in foreign banking or non-banking companies, other than those in joint ventures, which may be held to be part of their overall foreign banking operations. This report does not cover the appropriate supervisory treatment of these participations, but they should be taken into account by the relevant supervisory authorities.

2. General principles governing the supervision of banks' foreign establishments

Effective co-operation between host and parent authorities is a central prerequisite for the supervision of banks' international operations. In relation to the supervision of banks' foreign establishments there are two basic principles which are fundamental to such co-operation and which call for consultation and contacts between respective host and parent authorities: first, that no foreign banking establishment should escape supervision; and secondly, that the supervision should be adequate. In giving effect to these principles, host authorities should ensure that parent authorities are informed immediately of any serious problems which arise in a parent bank's foreign establishment. Similarly, parent authorities should inform host authorities when problems arise in a parent bank which are likely to affect the parent bank's foreign establishment.

Acceptance of these principles will not, however, of itself preclude there being gaps and inadequacies in the supervision of banks' foreign establishments. These may occur for various reasons.

First, while there should be a presumption that host authorities are in a position to fulfil their supervisory obligations adequately with respect to all foreign bank establishments operating in their territories, this may not always be the case. Problems may, for instance, arise when a foreign establishment is classified as a bank by its parent banking supervisory authority but not by its host authority. In such cases it is the responsibility of the parent authority to ascertain whether the host authority is able to undertake adequate supervision and the host authority should inform the parent authority if it is not in a position to undertake such supervision. In cases where host authority supervision is inadequate, the parent authority should either extend its supervision, to the degree that it is practicable, or it should be prepared to discourage the parent bank from continuing to operate the establishment in question.

Secondly, problems may arise where the host authority considers that supervision of the parent institutions of foreign bank establishments operating in its territory is inadequate or non-existent. In such cases the host authority should discourage or, if it is in a position to do so, forbid the operation in its territory of such foreign establishments. Alternatively, the host authority could impose specific conditions governing the conduct of the business of such establishments.

Thirdly, gaps in supervision can arise out of structural features of international banking groups. For example, the existence of holding companies either at the head, or in the middle, of such groups may constitute an impediment to adequate supervision. Furthermore, particular supervisory problems may arise where such holding companies, while not themselves banks, have substantial liabilities to the international banking system. Where holding companies are at the head of groups that include separately incorporated banks operating in different countries, the authorities responsible for supervising those banks should endeavour to co-ordinate their supervision of those banks, taking account of the overall structure of the group in question. Where a bank is the parent company of a group that contains intermediate holding companies, the parent authority should make sure that such holding companies and their subsidiaries are covered by adequate supervision. Alternatively, the parent authority should not allow the parent bank to operate such intermediate holding companies.

Where groups contain both banks and non-bank organisations, there should, where possible, be liaison between the banking supervisory authorities and any authorities which have responsibilities for supervising these non-banking organisations, particularly where the non-banking activities are of a financial character. Banking supervisors, in their overall supervision of banking groups, should take account of these groups' non-banking activities; and if these activities cannot be adequately supervised, banking supervisors should aim at minimising the risks to the banking business from the non-banking activities of such groups.

The implementation of the second basic principle, namely that the supervision of all foreign banking establishments should be adequate, requires the positive participation of both host and parent authorities. Host authorities are responsible for the foreign bank establishments operating in their territories as individual institutions while parent authorities are responsible for them as parts of larger banking groups where a general supervisory responsibility exists in respect of their worldwide consolidated activities. These responsibilities of host and parent authorities are both complementary and overlapping.

The principle of consolidated supervision is that parent banks and parent supervisory authorities monitor the risk exposure—including a perspective of concentrations of risk and of the quality of assets— of the banks or banking groups for which they are responsible, as well as the adequacy of their capital, on the basis of the totality of their business wherever conducted. This principle does not imply any lessening of host authorities' responsibilities for supervising foreign bank establishments that operate in their territories, although it is recognised that the full implementation of the consolidation principle may well lead to some extension of parental responsibility. Consolidation is only one of a range of techniques, albeit an important one, at the disposal of the supervisory authorities and it should not be applied to the exclusion of supervision of individual banking establishments on an unconsolidated basis by parent and host authorities. Moreover, the implementation of the principle of consolidated supervision presupposes that parent banks and parent authorities have access to all the relevant information about the operations of their banks' foreign establishments, although existing banking secrecy provisions in some countries may present a constraint on comprehensive consolidated parental supervision.

3. Aspects of the supervision of banks' foreign establishments

The supervision of banks' foreign establishments is considered in this report from three different aspects: solvency, liquidity, and foreign exchange operations and positions. These aspects overlap to some extent. For instance, liquidity and solvency questions can shade into one another. Moreover, both liquidity and solvency considerations arise in the supervision of banks' foreign exchange operations and positions.

(a) Solvency
The allocation of responsibilities for the supervision of the solvency of banks' foreign establishments between parent and host authorities will depend upon the type of establishment concerned.

For branches, their solvency is indistinguishable from that of the parent bank as a whole. So, while there is a general responsibility on the host authority to monitor the financial soundness of foreign branches, supervision of solvency is primarily a matter for the parent authority. The *dotation de capital* requirements imposed by certain host authorities on foreign branches operating in their countries do not negate this principle. They exist, firstly, to oblige foreign branches that set up in business in those countries to make and to sustain a certain minimum investment in them, and secondly, to help equalise competitive conditions between foreign branches and domestic banks.

For subsidiaries, the supervision of solvency is a joint responsibility of both host and parent authorities. Host authorities have responsibility for supervising the solvency of all foreign subsidiaries operating in their territories. Their approach to the task of supervising subsidiaries is from the standpoint that these establishments are separate entities, legally incorporated in the country of the host authority. At the same time parent authorities, in the context of consolidated supervision of the parent banks, need to assess whether the parent institutions' solvency is being affected by the operations of their foreign subsidiaries. Parental supervision on a consolidated basis is needed for two reasons: because the solvency of parent banks cannot be adequately judged without taking account of all their foreign establishments; and because parent banks cannot be indifferent to the situation of their foreign subsidiaries.

For joint ventures, the supervision of solvency should normally, for practical reasons, be primarily the responsibility of the authorities in the country of incorporation. Banks which are shareholders in consortium banks cannot, however, be indifferent to the situation of their joint ventures and may have commitments to these establishments beyond the legal commitments which arise from their shareholdings, for example, through comfort letters. All these commitments must be taken into account by the parent authorities of the shareholder banks when supervising their solvency. Depending on the pattern of shareholdings in joint ventures, and particularly when one bank is a dominant shareholder, there can also be circumstances in which the supervision of their solvency should be the joint responsibility of the authorities in the country of incorporation and the parent authorities of the shareholder banks.

(b) Liquidity

References to supervision of liquidity in this section do not relate to central banks' functions as lenders of last resort, but to the responsibility of supervisory authorities for monitoring the control systems and procedures established by their banks which enable them to meet their obligations as they fall due including, as necessary, those of their foreign establishments.

The allocation of responsibilities for the supervision of the liquidity of banks' foreign establishments between parent and host authorities will depend, as with solvency, upon the type of establishment concerned. The host authority has responsibility for monitoring the liquidity of the foreign bank's establishments in its country; the parent authority has responsibility for monitoring the liquidity of the banking group as a whole.

For branches, the initial presumption should be that primary responsibility for supervising liquidity rests with the host authority. Host authorities will often be best equipped to supervise liquidity as it relates to local practices and regulations and the functioning of their domestic money markets. At the same time, the liquidity of all foreign branches will always be a matter of concern to the parent authorities, since a branch's liquidity is frequently controlled directly by the parent bank and cannot be viewed in isolation from that of the whole bank of which it is a part. Parent authorities need to be aware of parent banks' control systems and need to take account of calls that may be made on the resources of parent banks by their foreign branches. Host and parent authorities should always consult each other if there are any doubts in particular cases about where responsibilities for supervising the liquidity of foreign branches should lie.

For subsidiaries, primary responsibility for supervising liquidity should rest with the host authority. Parent authorities should take account of any standby or other facilities granted as well as any other commitments, for example, through comfort letters, by parent banks to these establishments. Host authorities should inform the parent authorities of the importance they attach to such facilities and commitments, so as to ensure that full account is taken of them in the supervision of the parent bank. Where the host authority has difficulties in supervising the liquidity, especially in foreign currency, of foreign banks' subsidiaries, it will be expected to inform the parent authorities and appropriate arrangements will have to be agreed so as to ensure adequate supervision.

For joint ventures, primary responsibility for supervising liquidity should rest with the authorities in the country of incorporation. The parent authorities of shareholders in joint ventures should take account of any standby or other facilities granted as well as any other commitments, for example, through comfort letters, by shareholder banks to those establishments. The authorities in the country of incorporation of joint ventures should inform the parent authorities of shareholder banks of the importance they attach to such facilities and commitments so as to ensure that full account is taken of them in the supervision of the shareholder bank.

Within the framework of consolidated supervision, parent authorities have a general responsibility for overseeing the liquidity control systems employed by the banking groups they supervise and for ensuring that these systems and the overall liquidity position of such groups are adequate. It is recognised, however, that full consolidation may not always be practicable as a technique for supervising liquidity because of differences of local regulations and market situations and the complications of banks operating in different time zones and different currencies. Parent authorities should consult with host authorities to ensure that the latter are aware of the overall systems within which the foreign establishments are operating. Host authorities have a duty to ensure that the parent authority is immediately informed of any serious liquidity in-adequacy in a parent bank's foreign establishment.

(c)   Foreign exchange operations and positions
As regards the supervision of banks' foreign exchange operations and positions, there should be a joint responsibility of parent and host authorities. It is particularly important for parent banks to have in place systems for monitoring their group's overall foreign exchange exposure and for parent authorities to monitor those systems. Host authorities should be in a position to monitor the foreign exchange exposure of foreign establishments in their territories and should inform themselves of the nature and extent of the supervision of these establishments being undertaken by the parent authorities.

Basle
May 1983

Appendix 3—MEMORANDUM OF UNDERSTANDING BETWEEN THE SECURITIES ASSOCIATION (TSA) AND THE BANK OF ENGLAND (THE BANK) ON THE FINANCIAL SUPERVISION OF BANKS

1 This memorandum sets out the framework agreed between the Bank and TSA for the assessment and monitoring of the financial soundness of entities which are both authorised under the Banking Act 1987 and authorised under s. 7, Financial Services Act 1986, and which are incorporated in the UK (or UK partnerships). The arrangements reflect the recognition by TSA and the Bank of the desirability of avoiding the duplication of assessment of financial soundness and of its monitoring. They do not affect the statutory position under the Banking Act and the Financial Services Act that both authorities remain responsible for ensuring that each institution which it has authorised remains fit and proper.

2 On the application of a bank for authorisation by TSA, TSA will promptly notify the Bank of the application, and will discuss with the Bank whether the bank concerned is fit and proper from the point of view of capital adequacy, liquidity and other matters relating to financial soundness. In particular, TSA will need to be satisfied that the bank satisfies the capital adequacy requirement to which it will be subject after authorisation (see *The Requirements to be Applied in Different Cases*, on pp. 144–5).

3 If TSA proposes to grant the application, the bank concerned may apply to TSA for the TSA's financial regulation rules (as set out in Chapter III of TSA's rulebook) to be modified. If it appears to TSA that compliance with its financial regulation requirements in full would be inappropriate for the bank, having regard to the treatment of banking business under those rules and the supervisory requirements of the Bank, TSA and the Bank will agree the appropriate modified capital and reporting requirements which will apply to that bank.

TSA expects that in most, if not all, cases, these modified requirements would be those set out in categories (b) or (c), see pp. 144–5, according to the nature and scope of the investment business of the bank. TSA and the Bank will require adequate capital to be maintained at all times, and banks will be liable to spot checks between reporting dates.

All banks will remain subject to certain of the Financial Regulations (e.g. the rules concerning Accounting Records) and to all other rules, including the Conduct of Business Rules and Client Money Regulations.

Similarly, all banks will remain subject to all the Bank's requirements except where they are specifically modified under these arrangements. For example, all banks will remain subject to the Bank's requirements in respect of large exposures and liquidity.

4   In the great majority of cases (i.e. those falling in categories (b) and (c), see pp. 144–5), TSA and the Bank agree that the Bank should be 'lead regulator'. In these cases, the capital position of the bank will be monitored by the Bank in accordance with the agreed method of assessment as set out on pp. 144–5 and a quarterly report will be made by the Bank to TSA. This report will state whether or not the relevant requirement was satisfied at the quarterly date. It will also include a summary balance sheet and information relevant to the investment business being carried on by the bank.

TSA expects that, although these reports will no doubt sometimes give rise to queries which will need to be answered (which, where necessary, will be referred to the bank concerned by the Bank), they will normally be adequate in themselves to satisfy TSA that the bank is in compliance with the agreed requirement. In particular, TSA does not expect to need to know details of the bank's banking business as long as the agreed requirement continues to be satisfied.

In addition, banks which trade securities as principals will be required (other than in the *de minimis* case of category (c), see p. 145), to submit more detailed and more frequent returns[1] relating to the bank's securities positions in the same way as securities firms which are not banks. Such returns will be made to the Bank who will pass copies promptly to TSA.

5   If and when situations occur in which a bank begins to give rise to concern to either the Bank or TSA, there will be close

---

1. TSA rules require the submission of fortnightly securities position statements. Banks which are members of TSA will be required to make the same returns with the same frequency as other members of TSA who trade securities on their own account.

consultation and a much fuller sharing of information between the two authorities. In such cases TSA will need sufficient information to form a judgment whether action to protect the interests of investors is necessary and whether the bank remains fit and proper.

6   If, as lead regulator, the Bank at any time becomes aware that the relevant capital test has been, or is likely to be, breached, or material concerns otherwise arise relating to the bank's financial soundness, the Bank will immediately inform TSA. Similarly, TSA would inform the Bank if it was the first to become concerned, which might be the case, for example, where it was lead regulator of a bank falling in category (a), see p. 144, or where its concern was triggered other than through the regular monitoring of returns. Concerns which would be expected to give rise to consultation include (but would not be limited to):

—concerns about the liquidity position of the bank;
—concerns about control procedures of the bank which are relevant to the bank's investment business;
—concerns arising from supervisory visits, prudential interviews or reports of the bank's auditors;
—concerns arising from late or inaccurate prudential returns.

In such cases, and where the Bank is lead regulator, the Bank would establish the position with the bank concerned and discuss with the bank its plans. The Bank and TSA would then meet to consider the position. It is likely that in many such cases TSA would not need to know the full details of the position on the banking side, although it would need to know sufficient to be able to satisfy itself, taking into account the Bank's expertise in assessing problems on the banking side, that the necessary action was being taken. In the unlikely event of their not being of one mind as to the action to be taken, TSA would retain the right to act in accordance with its responsibilities and powers. This would include right of access to all information relating to the bank's business. However, in the case of any initial disagreement between the Bank and TSA on the necessary action, there would be urgent reference to senior levels in both organisations to try to seek an agreed view before any decision was made by TSA to intervene with a bank directly itself as a result of concerns relating to financial soundness.

7   In the early stages of operating these lead regulator arrangements, the senior officials of TSA and the Bank will meet periodically to review the effectiveness of the arrangements and any particular difficulties experienced. The framework set out in this memorandum and the detailed arrangements made under it will in any case be subject to regular review by TSA and the Bank (in consultation with the SIB).

THE REQUIREMENTS TO BE APPLIED IN DIFFERENT CASES

(a)   Banks whose business is almost exclusively securities or other investment business and where non-investment business is negligible.
In these cases, which are expected to be few, TSA expects to apply its Financial Regulations in full and not to modify those requirements except that the definition of capital will for all purposes be that defined by the Bank. Accordingly, the Bank expects not to apply its own risk asset ratio requirement. TSA and the Bank will agree in such cases whether it is more appropriate for TSA or the Bank to monitor compliance with those rules. However, where it is agreed that TSA will monitor compliance with those rules the Bank will continue to set guidelines for, and monitor, other aspects of the bank's business (including liquidity and large credit exposures, guidelines for foreign currency exposure and adherence to any monetary policy requirement).

(b)   Banks whose business includes both investment business and non-investment banking business and whose trading in securities as a principal requiring either authorisation or exemption under the Financial Services Act is more than a *de minimis* level.
In these cases, the Bank will be lead regulator but, for the purposes of the Bank's monitoring of the requirement for TSA the Bank's risk asset ratio assessment will be modified in two respects.
In addition to the normal risk asset ratio calculation for the bank as a whole there will be:

(i)   a parallel capital requirement relating to a bank's positions in securities requiring either authorisation or exemption under the FSA (including its primary market and underwriting positions). This will involve the calculation of the position risk requirement under TSA's Financial Regulations on securities trading positions, or, at the option of a bank which is also a listed money market institution and where the preponderance of securities trading business is exempt under s. 43 of the Act, in accordance with the Bank's 'grey book' weights (other securities positions, classified as banking assets, will continue to be subject to the appropriate weights laid down by the Bank);

(ii) a capital requirement for the counterparty risk requirement for counterparty balances arising from the acquisition of trading positions in instruments included under (i) above in accordance with TSA's Financial Regulations.

The aggregate of the amounts in (i) and (ii) above will then be taken together with the Bank's risk asset ratio requirement for all other assets and off-balance sheet items and measured against the capital base of the bank (as defined by the Bank). In these cases, only certain of TSA's Financial Regulations will apply.

(c) Banks whose trading in securities as a principal requiring either authorisation or exemption under the FSA is *de minimis*, but which nevertheless require authorisation under the Financial Services Act.

In these cases, the Bank will be lead regulator and will assess and monitor the Bank's capital requirement in accordance with its normal risk asset ratio assessment.

As in (b) above, certain of TSA's Financial Regulations will be disapplied.

In many cases it will be clear to which of a bank's securities positions it will be appropriate to apply this requirement; however, the Bank and TSA recognise that there will be a number of positions where it is not clear cut. In these cases, the scope of the requirement will be for the Bank to determine with the bank concerned, in accordance with principles agreed between the Bank and TSA and taking into account the accounting treatment of these positions.

INDEX

BANK—*contd.*
non-banking authorities,
supervision of *136*
joint venture, participation in
foreign *134*
Mareva injunction, breach of *25, 34*
monitoring exercises in suspicious
cases *85*
name, use of, by credit
institutions *119, 126*
new customer, liability for failure to
verify identity of *83*
overseas branches and subsidiaries,
development of *110*
police enquiries about customer *85*
postponement of obligation to
repay *93, 100*
repayment, methods of *104*
reputation, damage to *84*
residence of *54*
securities position, returns to Bank of
England and TSA, as to *142*
securities, trading in,
business almost exclusively *144*
de minimis trading in
securities *145*
supervision of, joint *115, 141*
set-off, right of, where Mareva
injunction *26*
subsidiary,
foreign, supervision of *134*
independent legal entity, as *1, 2,
134*
letter of comfort by foreign bank
to *2*
liquidity, supervision of *139*
solvency, supervision of *137*
supervision of,
investment and non-investment
business, where both *115, 141,
144*
securities business, where mainly
concerned with *144*
TSA Financial Regulations, subject
to *142, 144*
BANK ACCOUNT
current account set-off *58, 67*
drug trafficking, handling account
after reporting suspicions of *5,
88, 91*
jurisdiction,
branch, dispute due to operations
of *48*

BANK ACCOUNT—*contd.*
conditions based on cause of
action *48*
confirming bank, joinder of,
where letter of credit *49*
Convention, under 1968 *46*
service of writ or process out
of jurisdiction, conditions
for *51*
managed account arranged *103*
opening of, responsibility of bank
in *4, 79*
proper law of *3, 53, 102*
branch of bank, account at *54,
102*
credit or debit balance situated,
where *3, 53, 102*
residence of debtor *3, 54*
source of funds, duty to make
enquiries as to *6*
BANK DEPOSIT. *See also* BANK
ACCOUNT
account transfer, payment by *105*
agreement that repayment by any
branch *94*
branch where deposit kept,
localisation of obligation to repay
at *2, 94, 96*
cash, repayment in *104*
certificate of deposit *94, 96*
constructive trustee, liability of bank
as *5*
credit risk, liability of bank as a whole
to repay where *95*
debtor/creditor relationship between
parties *2, 94*
exchange control, effect of *93, 100*
expropriation of *93. See also*
EXPROPRIATION
recognition of foreign law *98–100*
freeze order in relation to *93, 101.
See also* FREEZE ORDER
lex situs of deposit debt *96, 101*
localisation of promise to pay at
branch where deposit kept *2, 94,
96*
moratorium in relation to *93, 100.
See also* MORATORIUM
payment, methods of *104*
proper law of banking contract *96,
101*
source of funds, duty to make
enquiries as to *6*

151